LORENZ

LORENZ

BREAKING HITLER'S
TOP SECRET CODE
AT BLETCHLEY PARK

CAPTAIN JERRY ROBERTS

The
History
Press

First published 2017

The History Press
The Mill, Brimscombe Port
Stroud, Gloucestershire, GL5 2QG
www.thehistorypress.co.uk

British Library Cataloguing in Publication Data.
A catalogue record for this book is available from the British
Library.

ISBN 978 0 7509 7885 9

Typesetting and origination by The History Press
Printed and bound in Great Britain by TJ International Ltd

A SELECTION OF TRIBUTES TO CAPTAIN JERRY ROBERTS

Captain Jerry Roberts MBE was a true gentleman and – to the last days of his long life – an outstanding ambassador for Bletchley Park. In World War Two he was a key member of the team who deciphered the most secret communications that changed the outcome of the war. Unfailingly modest about his own achievements, he was committed to the end to achieving recognition for the work of his colleagues and the contribution of all those who worked at Bletchley Park. He will be greatly missed. Our thoughts are with his devoted wife Mei.

Sir John Scarlett KCMG OBE, chairman of the Bletchley Park Trust, responding to the news of Jerry's death.

Jerry remained, into his high 80s and early 90s, a terrific speaker who could hold large audiences spellbound. His intelligence, humour and generosity endeared him instantly to all who knew him, whether slightly or well. He leaves his family, many friends and countless admirers worldwide.

Professor Susanne Kord, University College London (UCL).

Today Bletchley's fortunes have dramatically improved thanks, in no small measure, to Jerry's work on so many fronts. And so it was hardly surprising that Jerry, at the end of his life, was honoured several times for his historic achievements. Almost at the end, he wryly remarked to me; 'Funny thing Charles ... sixty years later I still find myself trying to "break" car number plates!'

Jerry, we all owe you a great debt, and we miss your smile and your hat!

Lord Charles Brocket, a friend of Jerry and Bletchley Park, TV presenter and journalist, talking at Jerry's memorial service at St Martin-in-the-Fields in London.

Jerry was an extraordinary man and he made a real impression upon me – I felt his presence and spirit every day that I worked on the 'Codebreakers' film. In fact, his honesty, attitude and belief in Bletchley – and his need to tell those stories – all combined to give that programme a moral core and sense of purpose and decency which made for something very special. As such it couldn't have existed without him and I hope it serves as one of many tributes to him.

Julian Carey, BBC film director and producer of the 2011 BBC *Timewatch* programme on the Lorenz story, 'Codebreakers: Bletchley Park's Lost Heroes'.

We all owe an immense debt of gratitude to you and your colleagues who worked tirelessly throughout the war to decode information vital to the Allied efforts. Your work helped not just to save lives, but to bring this dark period in our history to a swifter conclusion than could have been achieved without your efforts.

David Cameron (British prime minister, 2010–16), in a letter to Jerry Roberts on 21 November 2012.

DEDICATION

To my fellow codebreakers and colleagues in the Testery team at Bletchley Park, who broke every Lorenz code by hand until the end of the Second World War.

To Bill Tutte, in particular, who broke Hitler's Lorenz cipher system in 1942 without ever having seen this complex machine, which was vastly more secret and significant than Enigma.

To Tommy Flowers, who designed and built a machine called Colossus for speeding up the Lorenz codebreaking – this was the world's first ever electronic computer in 1944. We all owe a huge debt to his work for inventing the modern computer.

To all those men and women who worked at Bletchley Park where ciphers and codes were decrypted. Sadly, most of them are no longer with us and they have never received the recognition they deserved for their extraordinary achievements.

Finally, to my dear wife Mei, for her dedicated support of twenty-five years, without whom this book would not have been written.

CONTENTS

FOREWORD BY
PADDY O'CONNELL

They were often signed with the two initials A.H. – Adolf Hitler – and we received them for much of the war.

Jerry Roberts deciphered Hitler's most secret messages – and there were many others, too, between his top generals, all encrypted on the specially designed Lorenz machine. The information ended up not just in the German High Command where it was intended but on the desk of Winston Churchill too. Jerry yearned to reveal how, but as a codebreaker and a German linguist at Bletchley Park, he was sworn to secrecy for years. Then, as the story of the Enigma machine became much better known, this separate tale of the cipher nicknamed Tunny by the British often became confused in the public mind and merged into one.

It was a staggering achievement, as statistically impossible as it was unimaginable. Whilst this brainpower was later boosted by machines (specifically Colossus), much of it still was done by hand. Jerry wanted future generations to understand how key linguists, codebeakers, engineers, mathematicians and more worked together in a feat of reverse-engineering. The team at Bletchley cracked Lorenz without ever seeing the twelve-wheeled device.

Jerry worried that this risked being forgotten or misunderstood. He wanted to name the names of the key people involved, and to describe in detail how the information they mined was passed not just to Churchill but to the Allied commanders planning for D-Day and to the Russians too.

I met him many times with my mum, who was a Wren working at Bletchley Park. This is the account of one of those few men in life who wants all the others to get the credit. We promised him to help get this story told, and it's as humbling as it is an honour to write these few lines of introduction.

Paddy O'Connell, presenter BBC Radio 4 and BBC Radio 2, 2017

FOREWORD BY MEI ROBERTS

My husband Jerry Roberts died on 25 March 2014, aged 93, shortly after completing this memoir. BBC News and almost every major newspaper from *The Times* to *The New York Times*, national and international, featured a formal obituary.

During the final six years of his life, Jerry dedicated an enormous amount of time and effort to raising public awareness of Bletchley Park's major achievements on the Lorenz cipher, and the extraordinarily important work carried out by his team at Bletchley Park, much of which is still largely unknown to the public. He travelled extensively, giving public talks and working tirelessly for better recognition of his colleagues. Jerry was awarded an MBE in 2013, but he hoped that one day his whole team would be recognised for their contribution.

He was calm, humorous and a great character, with generosity and determination – an outstanding Englishman. I sorely miss his amazing and unique stories. I have such a vivid memory of Jerry talking with Her Majesty the Queen in July 2011 at Bletchley Park, recounting his experiences of breaking the Lorenz code. I heard him tell the Queen what it was like to read messages signed, 'Adolf Hitler, Führer', before they were even received by the German High Command in the field. Who else has stories like that?

Jerry was an amazing man and played a significant role in the war for his country and for Europe. He remained modest, despite his phenomenal achievements. His star will shine in the sky forever.

Sadness is never overcome, but the outpouring of recognition and admiration for him and his work have helped me through each day and made the sadness somehow easier to bear. On behalf of our family, I thank you all sincerely from the bottom of my heart.

Goodbye, my dear Jerry, may you rest in peace.

My heartfelt thanks to Margaret and Paddy O'Connell for introducing me to Heather Holden-Brown (HHB Agency Ltd) and for Heather's help in publishing Jerry's book.

Mei Roberts, 2017

In loving memory. A portrait of Jerry sketched by Mei

INTRODUCTION

Captain Jerry Roberts entered the ranks of the army as an officer in the early stages of the Second World War. Fluent in several foreign languages, he was a founding member and senior cryptographer in the Testery, the special unit at Bletchley Park tasked with the daily breaking of Lorenz (called Tunny by the British), the Nazis' highest-level communications cipher system, which was used between Adolf Hitler and his top generals in the High Command. Decrypts from Lorenz enabled British commanders to know what the Germans planned, and the decisions they made helped Allied forces to hasten the end of the Second World War by at least two years, saving tens of millions of lives. The work on breaking the Lorenz cipher also led directly to the development of the world's first electronic, programmable computer.

Following this remarkable start to his career, after Bletchley Park Jerry Roberts was a member of the War Crimes Investigation Unit in Europe (WCIU), where he helped to track down Nazi criminals and bring them to trial. When Jerry left the army, the Official Secrets Act prevented any discussion of his contribution to the war effort with both Bletchley Park and the WCIU. His career was slightly in the doldrums, until a chance encounter with an ex-colleague from Bletchley Park sparked a new and unexpected career in international market research. Roberts established the first market research company in Venezuela, and later set up his own companies in the UK and Europe.

In the final six years of his life, Roberts campaigned tirelessly to raise public awareness of the importance of the Lorenz story, which was declassified only at the beginning of this century. In contrast, Enigma became public in the 1970s. Lorenz had wrongly been overshadowed by the fervour surrounding Enigma, due to the highest levels of security imposed by the Official Secrets Act.

Jerry felt it was his duty to ensure his colleagues in the Testery received their rightful recognition, in particular Bill Tutte, who broke the extremely complex Lorenz cipher system without ever having seen the cipher machine. Tutte died in 2002, without receiving public recognition nor any award for his achievements. Tommy Flowers, who designed and built the Colossus, the world's first programmable electronic computer, died in 1998 – also without gaining any recognition.

At age 93, Roberts was the last surviving Lorenz cryptographer. He was honoured several times for his historic achievements in his final two years. This autobiography charts Roberts' long and varied life, simultaneously personal and historical. It is a first-hand account of virtually unknown twentieth-century history – a history that, without Roberts and his colleagues at Bletchley Park, might well have turned out very differently.

A BRIEF LEGACY OF BLETCHLEY PARK

Bletchley Park, once Britain's best-kept secret and home of the code-breakers, is today a heritage site and museum, with exhibitions, activities, events and attractions for visitors from all over the world. The Park's breathtaking Second World War codebreaking successes helped shorten the war and saved tens of millions of lives. After the war, General Eisenhower (later US president) said that Bletchley decrypts shortened the war by at least two years. Sir Harry Hinsley, one of the top codebreakers at Bletchley Park, also said the war had been shortened 'by not less than two years and probably by four years'.

Much of this was down to the work of Bill Tutte, who broke into the Nazis' highest-level cipher system, Lorenz SZ40/42 (codebreakers called it Fish or Tunny) and allowed codebreakers in the Testery to break those top-secret Lorenz codes – amounting to around 64,000 intelligence messages during the course of the war. Lorenz was only declassified at the beginning of the twenty-first century.

Bletchley Park was also the birthplace of Tommy Flowers' invention, the Colossus – the world's first programmable electronic computer – in 1944. Its only purpose at that time was to speed up one stage of the Lorenz codebreaking process and to try to win the war. Bill Tutte and Tommy Flowers changed the world, but then they disappeared from history because of the highest level of secrecy demanded by the government. There is an amazing replica of the wartime Colossus by Tony Sale and his team which can be seen today at the National Museum of Computing (TNMOC), housed in Block H at Bletchley Park.

During the Second World War, there were two major cipher systems worked on at Bletchley Park: Enigma and Lorenz. Most people have heard of Enigma and Alan Turing, but many have not heard of Lorenz or Bill Tutte. Lorenz was a vastly complex and much more significant cipher system in comparison to the well-known Enigma. Lorenz was kept under wraps by the Official Secrets Act for nearly sixty years after the war – whereas Enigma was kept secret for only thirty years. Bill Tutte and Tommy Flowers are the forgotten heroes of Bletchley Park.

Unlike Enigma, Lorenz carried only the highest grade of intelligence. Tens of thousands of Lorenz messages were intercepted by the British and broken by the codebreakers and linguists in the Testery at Bletchley Park. Messages were signed by only a handful of the German Army High Command, including Adolf Hitler himself.

Breaking into Lorenz gave the Allied High Command significant intelligence that changed the course of the war in Europe and saved tens of millions of lives at critical junctures, such as the Battle of Kursk in Russia and before and after D-Day. If the D-Day landings had failed, it would likely have taken at least two years to prepare for another major assault. Lorenz decrypts made a major contribution to winning the war.

There were three heroes at Bletchley Park: Alan Turing, who broke the naval Enigma that helped Britain not to lose the war in 1941; Bill Tutte, who broke the Lorenz system, which helped shorten the war; and Tommy Flowers, the father of the computer. Britain was extraordinarily lucky to have these three great men in one place during the darkest times of the Second World War.

Bletchley Park's success brought so many benefits to the British nation, and indeed to Europe as a whole. It also kick-started the modern computer industry, introducing us to the whole digital world of today. For years the wartime contribution of Bletchley Park has been totally undervalued. Only now is it beginning to be properly appreciated, but the story of what went on in the Testery is still largely unknown to many people.

Jerry Roberts, January 2014

PREFACE

This book is about my varied life, including my wartime experiences working at Bletchley Park as a cryptographer and linguist. It came about when my friend Professor Jack Copeland (the leading authority on Alan Turing) encouraged me to write a book about Lorenz and my involvement in it.

I'm very lucky to be alive today. I feel a great responsibility to help in spreading the word about Lorenz, especially for my fellow codebreakers and the support staff who worked with me in 'the Testery', the area of Bletchley Park where the codebreaking was done, named after its founder, Ralph Tester. As a team, we broke approximately 90 per cent of Hitler's top-level coded messages, around 64,000 in total – intelligence gold-dust! I recall their efforts and the contribution that they made, virtually unsung, unknown and unrecognised during their lifetime. Since 2007, I have been seeking better recognition for them, in particular for Bill Tutte.

I am now 93. As you can imagine, it is not easy to write a book at my age; my health and energy have slowed me down and I also have difficulty in writing clearly. I wish I could have started this book earlier. Luckily, with the great help of my wife, I have been able to record my text, and our daughter Chao typed it. It took some time to pull it all together, but it worked.

I would like to thank a number of people warmly for their help and kind contributions:

First, Philip Le Grand, the editor of *Bletchley Park Times* magazine (2006–13), who has done so much good work for Bletchley Park as a volunteer, always welcomed my articles about Lorenz and helped to revise the text.

Beatrice Phillpotts, a local journalist and editor who works for the *Haslemere Herald*, provided tremendous support and kept reporting on the Lorenz story to keep the campaign going.

Katherine Lynch, the media manager at Bletchley Park, a journalist and reporter of fine quality from the BBC, helped greatly to spread the word about the Lorenz story in various ways.

Rory Cellan-Jones, the BBC senior correspondent on technology in London, first recognised that Lorenz was an enormously significant piece of history.

Julian Carey, the producer from BBC Wales, made a BBC *Timewatch* programme in 2011, entitled 'Codebreakers: Bletchley Park's Lost Heroes', which told the full Lorenz story. The documentary received wide acclaim, in the UK and abroad.

Professor Susanne Kord, the head of the German department at UCL, set the ball rolling from the beginning, giving me a platform to speak publicly for the first time about the Lorenz story.

Lord Geoffrey Dear raised my subject to the House of Lords for Justice, but was rejected because it was felt that it should have been dealt with straight after the war.

I give my grateful thanks to all. I would also like to take this opportunity to thank many of those who supported me during my campaign for the last six years. This book is a personal record of my life. Any views expressed in it, of course, are my own. My aim is to keep the record as accurate as I can.

Jerry Roberts, January 2014

PART ONE

THE MAKING OF A CODEBREAKER

1

LIFE IN NORTH LONDON

I was born in November 1920, in a house called 'Morfa' in Wembley Park Drive, which is now opposite the main entrance to Wembley Stadium in north London. My parents had arrived in London in 1915 from Rhyl, North Wales. My elder brother Arnold had been born in Wales and was already 7 years old, and my younger brother Frank came along three and a half years after me; we were both born in London.

My father (Herbert Clarke Roberts) was a bank clerk, working in the Lloyds Bank head office in the City. He originally came from Liverpool and had trained as a pharmacist, but had to change his profession as the constant standing aggravated the varicose veins in his legs. He spent the rest of his working life travelling up to the City every day, until he retired at 65.

My mother, Leticia Frances Roberts (née Hughes), was a talented pianist. She played the piano in the chapel at Warren Road, Rhyl, and also sometimes the organ at St Asaph Cathedral nearby. In 1915, when the family moved to London, she left Rhyl with the thanks of the congregation and a handsome clock inscribed to her, 'Mrs H.C. Roberts, organist of Warren Road Chapel by friends and well-wishers on her leaving Rhyl, January 1915'. The clock still remains with me as a cherished possession. I also still have her beautiful mahogany piano stool with its engraved surround. It is the piece of furniture I am most attached to; within it are some of the sheets of music she used to play to us as children and to herself – she played the piano well.

Rhyl was where my mother was born and the family were originally located. Almost all of my mother's friends and relatives were from North Wales and we had uncles and aunts (some of whom we never saw) in Lancashire, Chester and Manchester, as well as Liverpool, where my father's side came from. We were one of the many families who gravitated towards London in search of better opportunities.

There was wholesale movement away from North Wales in the early years of the last century. One uncle went to Chester, where he worked for Crawford's, the biscuit company. Another uncle, Lou, went to work in the textile industry in Manchester. A third, John, came down to London, to Finchley, where he practised as a doctor. My Auntie Minnie, whose husband was killed in the Great War leaving her with two growing children Gwylmor and Nerys, took over a grocery store with a post office in Greenford, North Ealing. Auntie Minnie's husband was richer, and Gwylmor was able to buy a car, a relatively rare thing to own at that time, which gave him extra mobility and standing when he went into business and prospered. He also visited the US in the early 1930s when very few people made the trip.

There was yet one more refugee from Wales, our Uncle Edward. He was my mother's youngest brother. He had a speech defect but it did not prevent him from successfully running a tobacconist shop at Sudbury Hill in north-west London. He lived over the shop and added a second store a few years later. Eventually my mother's parents came down from Wales to live with him.

We always called them *Taid* (Welsh for grandpa) and *Nain* (grandma). Uncle Edward lived close to the tube station at Sudbury Hill, one stop from ours. We used to see them from time to time, as they lived nearby, about fifteen minutes' walk away. Taid was always impeccably dressed in a full suit, complete with buttoned-up waistcoat, and a silvery beard always carefully trimmed. Nain was rather heavily built; she invariably wore longish skirts of heavy and dark materials. The chapel was taken very seriously in those days; our family had closer ties to the chapel than most because my mother played the organ on Sundays for some years.

On my father's side, there was my grandfather Robert William Roberts and grandmother Maria Roberts (née Clarke). I never met Granny Clarke, but I heard a lot about her. I have a portrait of her (c. 1850) left to me by my parents. She looked a really formidable character – a true Victorian matriarch. She must have had quite a lot of authority and respect in the family. All of her sons and her grandsons (and us) carry her name – Clarke.

I also have an original newspaper cutting of one of her sons, Frank Roberts, from the front page of the *Daily Sketch* (the *Daily Sketch* merged with the *Daily Mail* in 1971), which is dated Friday, 9 January 1914 and entitled 'England may well be proud of these gallant officers', with an article by an American writer. Uncle Frank was a third officer of the Booth liner *Gregory* in the Royal Navy, based in Liverpool. The newspaper wrote that he was a hero. Apparently he dived into icy water and saved five Americans from the wrecked oil ship *Oklahoma*. He later transferred to the army and was killed in action in France in 1916. He was buried at the Woburn Abbey Cemetery at Cuinchy, between Béthune and La-Bassée in the Pas-de-Calais. He is a family member of whom we can truly be proud.

Recently, I came to know another relative from my father's side, my nephew John French and his wife Pam. I only came to meet them after they had seen me on TV. John's grandmother Madge was my auntie. I saw her a number of times, and I knew her daughter Peggy (my cousin) well when we were both teenagers. John is Peggy's son and as an engineer worked with a German firm based in Hampshire and has just retired aged 62. He has done a lot of work putting together the family tree and can trace the family back by five generations. It is quite fascinating to see how widespread a quite ordinary family can become.

In the old days, we hardly ever saw each other; you could hardly call our family close-knit. This was before the age of the family car and people simply did not move around as readily as they do today. You would have to go by bus or train (or both) and this could be very tiring and time consuming. Today we think nothing of driving hither and thither. This is one of the major differences in lifestyle from then to now, and it has had a huge effect.

The old Wembley Stadium in north London was built in 1923, three years after I was born in 1920. My elder brother Arnold recalled the open fields and woods which lay between our house and the River Brent before the stadium was built. The area must have become much noisier during the construction of the stadium. We had a small garden behind our house, but it stood immediately onto the street and this would no doubt have become much busier and noisier. As a result, my parents decided to move further out to Sudbury, a suburb of Wembley, 2 or 3 miles further away from central London.

The Wembley area had been largely developed already and Sudbury was the next open area in the north-west. The Piccadilly Underground line had pushed 10 miles or so further out to the west and railway stations were set at key points along the route. Around these, estates were soon built on green fields outside of Sudbury town and Sudbury Hill. New housing was put up and there was steady growth of the metropolis in this direction right up to the start of the Second World War, fifteen years later. The sheer area covered by new housing in this period was phenomenal. This was a familiar pattern as London expanded and people moved further out. The development of the Tube lines encouraged this and fostered the great outward growth of London.

Our father bought a new house at 18 Station Crescent in 1924 and we were to live there for the next twenty years or so. It was close to the Sudbury Town Underground station, three minutes' walk away, so he was able to easily commute up to the City. Later, I was to use the railway on a daily basis to get to Latymer in Hammersmith for my schooling.

The house itself was of semi-detached design, which was quite the fashion in housing development at that time. Many streets had been built on this pattern: two houses built as one unit with a space between that and the next double unit. I used to wonder why it was developed in this way, but I suppose the design allowed the family to go in through the back door, as well as through the front door. Later, it proved even more useful because in the 1950s and 1960s many people put in a garage to house the family cars which had become so popular after the war.

We had a back garden, but it was always in the shade, cold and unfriendly. The front of the house and garden got all the sun. Our real back garden was Horsenden Hill, an open space six or seven minutes' walk away from our house. The top of the hill itself was fifteen minutes or so away. This was the only space that remained green in our area. The Grand Junction Canal flowed a further ten minutes away. My younger brother Frank and I used to play in the woods and fields on the lower slopes round Horsenden Hill, with endless games of football and cricket using two trees as goal posts and one tree as the stumps. The hill was very pleasant territory, and if you went over the top and far enough down the other side you would come to the Grand Junction Canal and see horses on the towpath pulling barges behind them. The bargemen on board would give us a wave. At another point, near the top of the hill, the grass had been worn away. There were two or three tea trays that kids like us used to slide down the hill on. Nobody ever walked off with those tea trays – they were part of our heavenly playground on the hill.

Another reminder of the nineteenth-century mode of life was provided by an establishment 50 yards away from our house at that time. This was a smithy run by a full-time blacksmith. There was still a substantial need to shoe horses and to carry out other kinds of metalwork.

It is strange to realise the scope and pace of the changes in London over the last century. In the lifetime of one man, who still remembers the situation, the area we lived in just after the First World War changed enormously.

HOLIDAYS

Every summer our parents would take us children to the seaside for two or three weeks. At first, this meant Bournemouth. In later years, we went to Minehead and Sandown on the Isle of Wight; always where there were sandy beaches. These were greatly enjoyable. We built sandcastles, played ball games on the sand and splashed about in the sea. My father, usually wearing a summer suit in light grey, would smoke either a pipe or cigarettes. However, he never paddled; he was probably worried about showing his legs with the varicose veins. My mother always wore a summer dress or skirt with stockings, which she would never take off in public, so she never paddled either. In those days, people were much more conservative about what they wore on the beach; even men's swimming costumes usually went up to the chest. Everybody, including children were much more covered up.

We used to go on the kind of excursions common to such places. At Sandown, for instance, we went to Osborne House, and it was there that I started to take an interest in our country houses. My love of these often fine historic houses which survive to this day is now shared by my wife Mei, who has a great interest in the historical side of our country. Indeed, we have both taken great enjoyment when we make trips or even just see them on the television. We both enjoy the countryside and country towns.

LIFE AT HOME

Monday was wash day every week and it was physically an extremely taxing job. My mother had a peaceful, equable nature, but it was as well not to cross her on Mondays! The process began by setting up a copper in the kitchen. This was a large, round tub, about 3ft high and 2½ft across. The clothes were put in and water poured in from kettles – a small amount of cold, but mostly hot. They then had to be stirred around with a 'dolly stick' and, of course, they became very heavy as the water soaked into them. When this process had been thoroughly completed, any remaining dirty bits on the clothes were rubbed over with soap (no soap flakes at that time) and thoroughly rinsed. The clothes were then lifted out one by one and rinsed out with fresh cold water from the tap in the sink, then rung out and hung up in the garden. This had to be done for all the clothes that needed washing: shirts, underpants, even bed sheets, tablecloths and so on. Nowadays, wash days are made lighter by throwing everything into the washing machine. This is just one example of how daily labour has been made easier in the home during the last seventy years or so.

After my homework, I used to help my mother from time to time with her work in the kitchen. I also used to help with the shopping sometimes. On Saturdays we liked to have Sainsbury's sausages for lunch, so I had to walk all the way to the supermarket and buy a pound of sausages for the family. I loved to buy the butter. The counter assistant had a huge slab of butter in front of him and two wooden paddles. With these, he would carve off just the right amount and pat it into shape before wrapping it up. It was fun to watch his wonderful dexterity and speed.

I was usually very happy to make a contribution to help my mother because she had so much to do with the family and three boys. My elder brother Arnold did not pitch in on this; he was usually out and about with his mates. They formed a group which nowadays would probably be called a gang, but they never got involved in vandalising cars or property or any other mischief. I used to see very little of Arnold as he was always off and away.

I saw a lot more of my younger brother Frank. I was very close to him because I looked after him and played with him as he was three and a half years younger than me. We used to sleep in the same bed. I took the initiative in the games that we played before we went to bed. We were supposed to go to sleep at once, but most nights I would make up stories with him and he would play his part in whatever went on, but he had few initiatives – they all came from me! I loved acting things out to make him laugh. It was a good exercise of the imagination. However, sometimes my parents did not agree – they wanted us to go to sleep! When our voices went on too long there would be menacing shouts up the stairs. If we still continued then, instead of my mother, it would be my father shouting up the stairs. That always produced peace and quiet. My parents did not punish us, although they exercised their authority nonetheless and had little trouble with any of us.

On Sunday mornings in the winter, while my parents enjoyed a lie-in, I used to light the sitting room fire using balls of newspaper and sticks bought from the grocer. The other rooms remained unheated. I must have been 8 or 9 years old and Frank 5 or 6. Nowadays we just flick a switch on the central heating, gas fire or electric fire – it's much easier!

SCHOOLING

My schooling started at age 6. First, it was at Eton College (not quite the public school, but a tiny private school in Eton Avenue, Sudbury, in north-west London). I used to go to and from the school each day by myself, ten minutes each way. I still remember the roads I went through – quite simple and straight – past the Grand Central railway station, where the trains were still pulled along by steam engines; it was fascinating to see.

The school was run by Ms Dutton and I still remember she suffered from mild rhinitis and was always delicately dabbing her nose with a handkerchief. There were roughly thirty girls there and six boys, of which I was one. Amazingly, I was to meet up with one of them, Arthur Hall, when I went to live in a boarding house in Aberystwyth thirteen years later at UCL.

After this short spell at Eton College, when I was 7 my parents moved me to Wembley College, another private school run by headmaster, Mr Topliss. He taught us geography, but nothing else. Most of the rest of our education was down to Mr Fairbairn, the first of a series of really good teachers I was fortunate enough to have. He took most of the other subjects and did a very good job of interesting us in whatever we were learning. Mr Topliss, who normally sported a ginger-coloured suit with plus fours, ran the school but made little contribution to the teaching.

We normally had a fifteen-minute walk to school and then back at the end of the school day. Occasionally, our milkman would kindly give me a lift to the school in his Trojan milk float. This had solid rubber wheels and, as a result, the 400 bottles would make a terrible din, so that when I got off I was quite stupefied. The noise was made worse by the fact that the road had tramlines set in stone bricks.

Wembley College was a modest-looking establishment: a mid-sized suburban house, adapted to make two or three classrooms and educating between sixty and seventy students. Next door was the headmaster's house, so he could keep regular control of what was happening in the school. I did well at the college and was given substantial encouragement: I won prizes each year. I still have one of these, a book with the arms of the school handsomely embossed on the front in gold. The book itself – *Silas Marner* by George Eliot – was just about the least appropriate book to give an 11-year-old boy. I haven't actually managed to read it all, even now, but I am still proud of it.

This kind of encouragement must have helped me realise that it was worthwhile working hard for the future. At any rate, my parents must have been convinced that I was worth backing because they put me up for a scholarship at Latymer Upper School in Hammersmith, west London. If I could win that, it would be a very useful support financially, because I would have a grant to pay the fees which amounted to the princely sum of £6 each term. Fortunately, I did win the scholarship and started at Latymer in 1933.

2

LATYMER UPPER SCHOOL

I gained the scholarship and spent the next six years at Latymer, from 1933 until 1939. I made substantial progress on all subjects. Latymer was a first-class private boys' school and I had excellent teachers. I still remember with gratitude Mr Gregory, who taught me German and French. I made huge progress in both languages, and this prepared me to take a course in German and French at University College London (UCL) later on.

In comparison to Wembley College, at Latymer classes were a very much more serious affair and there was a relatively strict discipline imposed. In spite of that, the teaching was excellent and enjoyable. We wore a uniform with the school badge on the breast pocket, similar to today. I always enjoyed my studies and I have never been able to understand why so many boys did not react well to teaching and mucked about – it is a mystery to me. We had more subjects to deal with at Latymer School – art, scripture, history and German were added to our curriculum.

There was also a lot more scope on the sport side. I have many memories of the sports ground at Shepherd's Bush, where Latymer had its own playing fields, and I joined in on the cricket team. It was difficult for me to take part in football because, like my brother Frank, I had a poor chest and would be wheezing heavily after a few minutes. There were no 'puffers' (inhalers) in those days to bring relief. Nonetheless, I went on to become the school captain in cricket and did well both as a batsman and a bowler. I remember, in particular, there was an annual match of the first XI boys against a team made up of the teachers, and the boys won! I took part in the match against the teachers, which was always the most interesting event, although if you were bowling you had to be careful not to send down fast snorters to teachers who might then take it out on you when you got back to the classroom!

I continued to do well in my classwork, and when it came to the end of my schooldays I qualified for a place at University College London. UCL is one of the top three universities in the UK and probably the best for modern languages. Before I went to UCL, my mother had a brilliant idea. She arranged for me to spend six weeks in Germany to practise my German. She booked me into a German boarding house in Bad Godesberg, near Cologne. This was a quiet spa town on the River Rhine. There were no English-speakers, which was immensely valuable because I was obliged to speak German all the time with the other people in the house. My ability in the language improved in leaps and bounds.

After two weeks, my mother left me in the safe hands of Frau Becker, a lady of approximately 50 years of age who ran the guest house. There were five or six other guests, including Herr Kaufmann, a retired banking executive of 70 years. I was then 18 and we did not have much common ground. Nonetheless, it was helpful to speak with him. I used to go for walks with him along the Rhine and in the pleasant town. Another guest was a very different cup of tea: a young man of about 25 and one of the typical Nazis who supported Hitler fanatically. He seemed to make the others very uncomfortable with his views, though none of them dared to raise any objections as he would have reported them to the Gestapo and they would have suffered the consequences.

At that time, however, Hitler was doing seemingly extraordinary and praiseworthy things, raising the country by its bootstraps. This was the best period of his rule, in 1938. I was greatly saddened when war was actually declared in 1939, because it seemed such a point-less exercise. In the end, the war finished in 1945 and cost roughly

10 million lives every year – a total of 55 million people died in Europe. That was the price we paid for Hitler's rule.

However, there was little or no sign of that in 1938 while I was in Germany. Relations were friendly between the English and German people, and I was treated very well by the members of the household and Frau Becker.

When I got back home, I was in good shape to start my degree course at UCL. Thanks to my mother's initiative and her far sight, after six weeks of German practice I had gained a great deal of confidence. I left London a schoolboy and when I came back I would be a university graduate.

3

UNIVERSITY COLLEGE LONDON

By now, it was the summer of 1939. Because of the German threat to London, my college at UCL was evacuated to Aberystwyth ('Aber'), on Cardigan Bay in Wales, where one of the colleges that made up the University of Wales at that time was based. A number of the students grumbled about the move because they had got used to the fleshpots of London.

At Aber I had my first experience of living away from home and I had to find a place to live. Luckily, the milkman had come up trumps and recommended the boarding house of Miss Edwina John. In late September 1939 I made my way by train from London to Shrewsbury and from there through the lovely countryside of Mid Wales to Aber. Miss John turned out to be a smallish, dark Welsh lady of uncertain age; she was likeable and clearly would stand no nonsense. Her home was a large house in Portland Street, two streets away from the seafront. The atmosphere was sensible and friendly, and the boarders pretty heterogeneous.

A permanent fixture in the house was Mrs Thomas, a very pleasant silver-haired lady in her early 70s and a great knitter. The other inhabitants were quite a rich mixture. Another resident was Arthur Hall – a remarkable coincidence, since we had both been at the same school at Eton College when we were just 6 years old. We were two of the six boys lost among thirty girls, but had seen nothing of each other in the intervening twelve years – an extraordinary reunion! Now at UCL at the same time, he was studying law and I was studying languages, but we had little to do with each other.

Another paying guest was Steven Henry Harvey. He was an extraordinary character. A large, broad-beamed student in his last year as a postgraduate studying for his PhD in chemistry. He was very outgoing and almost every comment he uttered was downright funny: I have never in the rest of my life come across anyone who was such amusing company.

There was another student, William Butler (nicknamed 'Buttles'), with the exact opposite character of Steven Henry Harvey. He was taciturn and saturnine-looking, tall, with a serious demeanour, dark in appearance and spirit and yet not a depressing presence – another extraordinary contrast!

By further contrast, there was Misha, an unlikely and incongruous person to find in Mid Wales. He was exiled from Russia and we never knew his second name. He was about 40 years old and a scientist who worked at the National Chemical Laboratory at the back of Aber. He was rather taciturn; he didn't speak very much, and to me he seemed rather sardonic about the strange English and Welsh people amidst whom he had found himself. He would never speak about his past life in Russia and I always suspected he and his family had suffered bad times there.

It was a very pleasant and peaceful atmosphere in which to study. We all had separate rooms and so I was able to work hard and long hours. This was very necessary because I had to take my exams in summer 1941, thus having only two years in which to do the full three-year course.

I was fortunate to have good teachers, led by Professor Leonard Willoughby. He was the archetypal professor – 60ish, with a halo of silvery hair and a placid but very positive temperament. The professor was later to be the first major influence on the direction of my life stream towards Bletchley Park.

The life we lived at Aber was curiously detached from the life in London: I had no daily newspaper, there was no TV news and I had no radio to listen to for a source of news. We did not feel the danger the country was facing in the same way or to the same degree as Londoners. It was almost as though those events were happening in some foreign land. Of course, I returned to London for much of the holidays and was brought up to speed with the true situation then. But this was only for short spells and the only long holiday was the summer break in 1940.

A RURAL EPISODE

During the university holiday in 1940 a high proportion of able-bodied men entered the forces, and so male labour was short. It was crucial to get the harvest in and I volunteered to help. I spent eight weeks on a farm in Shropshire stacking 'stooks' (a circle of cut grain stalks bound together and placed on the ground in the field) and doing other kinds of quite hard labour, including picking potatoes, which involved a great deal of back bending. Through that summer we had fine weather every day from 8 a.m. to near 6 p.m. We had sandwiches brought to us as we toiled in the fields. We slept in the farmhouse, a large, ample building in the country style, and we were given minimal wages, which was the norm.

The machine harvester, in those days, would cut the corn, bind it and then throw it on the ground. It could not stay there, though; the sheaves had to be stacked in stooks, four or six being stood up and leaned against each other. If this were not done and it rained, the crop would be spoiled and never have a chance to ripen fully in the sun. Britain needed every scrap of food in 1940, as the U-boats were sinking so many of our food supply ships from America and Canada.

It was a hard and long working day. We were not used to it, but it was in its own way enjoyable. The peaceful, beautiful Shropshire countryside, the open air, the sunshine, the companionship of other workers and the feeling of doing a useful job for the country all contributed to a very positive experience. The farm workers themselves stood off initially from us city boys, but as they could see we were doing a good job and putting our backs into it they mellowed and we were better accepted.

The large old farmhouse belonged to Mr Stephen Ward. He had six sons. The five grown-up ones already had their own farms and the youngest was 16 years old – but there are no prizes for guessing what he was going to become when he grew up. There was one daughter, aged 25 or so. And guess what her husband did for a living? He, of course, was yet another farmer.

Mrs Ward ran the house with great authority, providing meals for all the menfolk. We lived in the main house on the farm, a large, old, comfortable building which in earlier days would have housed servants, gardeners and so on. We had our meals together in the big kitchen.

This lasted eight weeks and, in its own way, was extremely enjoyable. But the time soon came for me to return to my family in London, briefly, before going back to Aber by train.

Later, in the spring of 1941, I cycled out from Wembley to Aber along the 200 miles each way, which I spread over four days, staying in youth hostels. They cost 1 shilling per night, equivalent to 5p today, with breakfast included. The hostels were simple but comfortable. I had bought myself a bicycle which, though not a racing model, was lightweight and had drop handlebars. It was a very effective transport – so much so that I did it a second time, stopping this time in different towns along the way. The roads in those days were comfortable, with not many cars, because few people had cars or the petrol coupons with which to purchase fuel, unless they had special circumstances, such as being a doctor (though of course there were some who bought the coupons on the black market).

I enjoyed the cycling trip, except for the Welsh mountains which were fairly tough going. It was a very pleasant way of getting to know the country better, even if it was a stiff grind up the Welsh hills. In this manner, I had more genuine contact with the country in those four days of cycling than in all my previous years. I came to know there was more to Britain outside London and greatly enjoyed the experience.

THE UCL CURRICULUM: GERMAN AND FRENCH

At UCL we focused on the grammar of German and the structure of the language. We were also introduced to and made considerable study of German literature, which has given me pleasure ever since. At first, we studied the classical writers, including Lessing, Goethe and Schiller, and later, the romantic writers, particularly the poet Heine. At the same time, we learned a lot about the British poets – Alexander Pope, Wordsworth, Shelley, Keats, Byron and the rest – because Britain had undergone the same development, from classical to romantic, as Germany had.

I still quite often find myself reading poems of that period, although I have to confess it is mostly the romantic poets rather than the classical. Lessing's plays, for example, I find almost unreadable now. Even Alexander Pope, with his long epics, I find similarly difficult to assimilate. But the romantic poets, Wordsworth and the others, speak in terms that ordinary mortals can understand and appreciate. Even somebody new to literature would find immediate pleasure in reading their works, which is more than you can say about most of the classical writers.

Our tutor was Professor Leonard Willoughby, a distinguished scholar. He himself looked a bit like Goethe, and he specialised in the poet's works, on whom he had written a number of books. He managed to bring out a true appreciation of the beauties of the German language, as used by the romantics.

There is one additional benefit that came from studying the romantics. The composer Schumann wrote possibly the finest song cycle ever composed when he took a number of Heine's poems and set them to music for baritone and piano. Each poem is fitted to highly appropriate, extremely melodic music and anyone who speaks German is highly recommended to try to hear the work. As a result of this, I started reading the English romantic poets, particularly Byron. I only hope, though, that visitors do not associate me too strongly with Byron, who was described by a contemporary as 'mad, bad and dangerous to know' – hardly a recommendation! It was at this time that I began to enjoy classical music.

At school and university I had always been good at languages. I had a very good teacher at Latymer, Mr Gregory, and now Professor Willoughby, who greatly extended my knowledge of German and German literature. Being in Aber without distraction, I was able to concentrate pretty well on German and French.

Overall, it was a greatly enjoyable time at Aber, even if it was hard work. Although I was taught by the staff of UCL, I never actually set foot in the place; I had no contact at all with Gower Street in London. The first time I did go there was when I gave a talk to UCL students in November 2008, and again in their theatre in March 2009, entitled 'My Top-Secret Codebreaking during the Second World War'.

PART TWO

DOING MY BIT FOR THE WAR: 1941–45

4

RECRUITED TO BLETCHLEY PARK AS A CRYPTOGRAPHER

In the late summer of 1941 I received two letters which were to have a profound impact on my life. The first came from UCL and it told me that for my degree course in German and French I had been awarded an Upper Second – not bad, considering that I had had to do the three-year course in only two years in order to get permission to defer my military service. The second letter was from the War Office and summoned me to go up to Whitehall in London to attend an interview with a Major Masters. I was excited by the prospect, but wondered what it could all be about. Why did they choose me? Something to do with my German, I guessed.

A few days later, I was somewhere in the bowels of the War Office in Whitehall. Major Masters was using his prime technique to see whether I would be a suitable candidate for a job in intelligence. The major was from an army regiment, a trim, dapper man who spoke crisply. At the beginning of our meeting, he asked me to sign the Official Secrets Act. I signed it, but was not told the reason why (I suppose I am still bound by it all these years after the war!). Major Masters then went on to ask questions to do with my character and my background. He asked about my family. I told him about my parents, including my father's work in the City. He also checked my degree performance and asked how well I felt I spoke German and French. I was able to reassure him on all these points; for Major Masters' purposes, I was to find out later, this was an impeccable background.

After that, he asked me questions about my intellectual interests.

Major Masters: 'Do you play chess?'

Me: 'Yes, I enjoy a game of chess.'

Major Masters: 'Do you do puzzles, crossword puzzles for instance?'

Me: 'Oh, yes. I often wrestle with the one in the *Observer*, a medium-to-difficult.' I used to tackle the *Observer* crossword every Sunday; this was quite a difficult puzzle at the time and fairly taxing.

He seemed reasonably satisfied with the way the interview had gone and it closed with friendly handshakes; it had lasted thirty minutes. When I later compared notes with Peter Ericsson, who joined Bletchley Park with me at the same time, he had been asked the same questions but he gave rather different answers.

'Do you play chess?'

'No, no, no, not interested.'

'Do you do crosswords?'

'No, no, never, complete waste of time.'

In the end Peter and I were both accepted. In trying to foresee how useful a person might be at breaking ciphers, the recruiters saw any tendency to be good at chess or the better kind of crossword puzzles as promising. In fact, Peter and I were both recommended by the tutor at university – a personal recommendation was important – so we both ended up being accepted whether we were interested in chess and crosswords or not!

Peter and I were almost like twin brothers. We were both aged 20, went into the army on the same day and became founder members of the same unit – the Testery – at Bletchley Park. We performed the task of message breaking with equal success. If Major Masters' technique seems a little questionable, at least his conclusions were right – and a good deal more effective than his technique!

The body for which Major Masters was recruiting was the top-secret Government Code and Cipher School (GC&CS) at Bletchley Park, responsible for all the efforts to break every possible communication sent by the German Army, Navy and Air Force. The success of the work was crucial and in many vital situations made the difference between cataclysmic defeat at the hands of Hitler's Nazi regime and the survival of Britain.

Bletchley Park, 50 miles north-west of London in the heart of Buckinghamshire, was the home of the codebreakers: the most secret place in Britain. It was at this time that Bletchley began to bring young and talented people together from all over the country, to recruit the best and brightest they needed in order to tackle the problem of breaking into the enemy's communications, and to read the Germans' secret messages from their cipher machines – Enigma and, later on, the Lorenz SZ40/42.

The new Lorenz machine was the most sophisticated code machine the world had ever seen. The Germans were convinced that these machines could never be broken. As Britain entered the darkest days of the war, the need to unravel the secrets from these machines was ever greater.

During the Second World War, the kind of cipher systems Germany used were much more complex, more advanced and substantially more difficult to break than in the First World War. This was mainly due to the greater use of machines in the Second World War. This change started with the introduction of the Enigma machine in 1923 and was pushed further by various new machines, including the much more complex and most important German cryptographic system, Lorenz SZ40/42, a new high-grade cipher machine with twelve wheels. This was the machine I worked on and which we called Fish or Tunny. In order to break Fish, an excellent knowledge of the German language on the part of the cryptographer was essential.

It is quite extraordinary just how tightly security was maintained on Lorenz at Bletchley Park, not only during the war, but also for nearly sixty years after, it only being declassified at the beginning of this century. Even when I met Roy Jenkins in 1999, a fellow codebreaker who had been in the Testery, we still did not talk about the work of those days. Security at Bletchley Park was a top priority and one kept to one's own job and did not ask about other people's work, take notes or mention anything to anyone.

How was the selection process undertaken at Bletchley Park when they needed talented young people so urgently? Major Masters had a tough job on his hands. He needed German-speakers badly, but that was just the easy part. It was essential that people should not only be bright but also have good character. Recommendations were of extra importance in the hiring of personnel for Bletchley as it was almost impossible to sack any person for fear they might subsequently prejudice security.

In the early stages at Bletchley Park, mathematicians and German-speakers were urgently needed for all sorts of purposes. There was great pressure to find them. The logical places to look for them were the universities, which provided a natural hunting ground for young, bright students. A fair proportion of the senior figures at Bletchley Park were recommended and recruited from the top universities, mainly from Oxford, Cambridge and London. Bletchley railway station was a good connection point, running east, west, north and south, and Oxford, Cambridge and London are all within a thirty- to fifty-minute train ride. These top universities were rated by most people as the best in the country.

It will be seen that the Testery recruited primarily mathematicians and linguists to form the cryptographic staff. Senior people and graduates in both fields were contacted at the major universities and recommendations sought. In our unit, Peter Hilton and Roy Jenkins both hailed from Oxford University, but they were not linguists. Peter was a mathematician who taught himself some rudimentary German. Denis Oswald was also an Oxford man and taught German at a well-known public school in Uppingham. Peter Ericsson was recommended by his tutor at Oxford, because he spoke German in his family. Bill Tutte came from Cambridge.

I was accepted to work at Bletchley Park because I could speak fluent German. I think my tutor, Professor Willoughby, must have recommended me to the intelligence people in London. He had an intelligence background himself during the First World War, having broken German naval ciphers. This was a pretty important activity and he had worked in the famous Room 40 in Whitehall. This was the

British codebreakers' unit, the main cipher-breaking unit of the First World War and the precursor to Bletchley Park.

Recently, I learned that a fellow student at UCL, Mavis Batey, had also been recommended to intelligence by Professor Willoughby one year earlier than I. She entered UCL, but she did not want to leave London to go to Aberystwyth, preferring to do something to support the war effort. She was one of the very few female codebreakers at Bletchley Park and she worked on Enigma, as used by the Italian Navy, under Dilly Knox (she was one of 'Dilly's girls'). She went back to UCL after the war to finish her German course.

Another couple of weeks passed following the interview with Major Masters. I then received a further letter with a return rail ticket to Bedford, where the GC&CS ran a training course in basic cryptography. I was sent there for six weeks to learn the rudiments of codebreaking. This mainly consisted of simple hand ciphers. I found the course was very interesting, but it was not much practical help when I came to deal with Lorenz or even Double Playfair – a much simpler kind of hand cipher. It did not touch at all on the kind of machine ciphers that I was later to wrestle with when I reached Bletchley.

I learned in 2012, from Captain Arthur Maddocks, a colleague of mine in the Testery, that he went to the same training school in 1944. He went to Bletchley three years later than I. The course he undertook was quite different and included a section on the Lorenz cipher, despite Arthur being a wheelsetter rather than a message breaker. Wheelsetters also practised a small element of breaking, when they had to extend the original break-in in a handful of places (characters, letters or spaces), to keep their wheelsetting going, unlike we codebreakers who had to break many more (anything up to fifty consecutive places of the German cipher text at the first place).

I returned from Bedford and awaited events. Another letter came with instructions to go to Bletchley Park and meet with a Captain Tester (later Major). After a few days, I turned up at the sentry-guarded gates of the country house at Bletchley Park. When I passed through, I made my way to the house: a Victorian mansion set in pleasant grounds. The house was beautiful but slightly strange, and a real mixture of architectural styles. I came to like the building, which was quite unique-looking, with a small lake in front and quite a piece of land surrounding the mansion house.

Bletchley Park had been owned by a wealthy stockbroker called Herbert Leon since 1883, when he had bought a 300-acre piece of land and built the mansion as one of his family homes, but it was put up for sale at the end of the 1930s after the deaths of Sir and Lady Leon. However, in 1938 the government intervened and took it over for military intelligence purposes. Bletchley Park was already well connected, being at a junction of major roads and railways – a perfectly safe place for the government intelligence to hide away from London. In August 1939, Bletchley Park became the wartime GC&CS – the home of the codebreakers. It was given the cover name Station X.

The first person I met at Bletchley was Captain Ralph Tester. I was introduced to him as the person I would work with to set up a new unit, called the Testery. In fact, we were both recruited to Bletchley Park at the same time. I was to work with him for all that time, from autumn 1941 to the end of the war in 1945. Captain Tester, an urbane pipe smoker, was about 40 years old. He spoke excellent German, but was no cryptographer, nor did he pretend to be. He joined from Unilever, where he had enjoyed management experience. He returned to Unilever after the war.

At that time the Park continued to look like a park, well planted with trees and with a small lake on which there were ducks. Soon after I arrived, they began to build the huts, which looked like temporary structures but eventually came to occupy a lot of the grounds. They had to be built pretty quickly in order to accommodate more and more people later on in the war.

The intelligence units were quickly established in their various huts. Prosaic as they looked, the huts had an aura about them, such as might be attached to the vaults of the Bank of England. Bletchley Park, after all, was the site of the concentration of the most secret material in the country. When I started at the Park in 1941, there were only a few hundred people. Towards the end of the war, there were around 10,000.

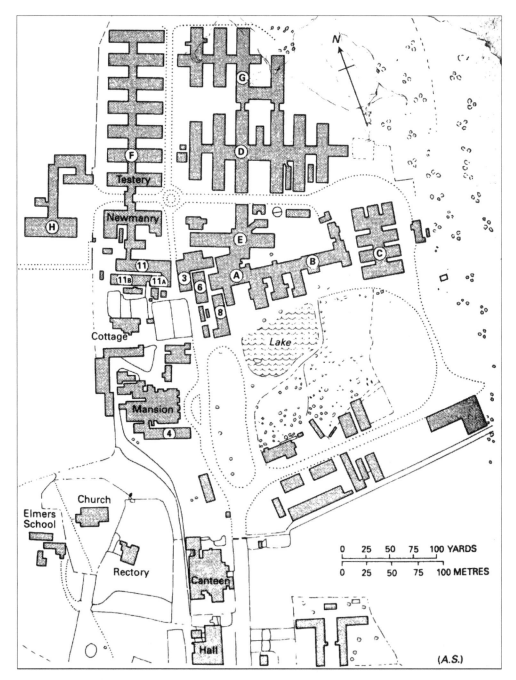

Bletchley Park layout 1939–45. The Testery was in Block F. From 1941 onwards, I saw the number of huts increase substantially. The Testery team moved twice. We started in the Mansion, then moved out to a temporary Hut 15a (near the end of the tennis courts) and from mid-1943 onwards the Testery and the Newmanry settled in Blocks F (and H) until the end of the war.

5

ESTABLISHING THE TESTERY IN 1941

When I arrived at Bletchley Park in autumn 1941, four of us set up the new unit called the Testery, named after Captain Ralph Tester, who was the oldest of us and the team leader. The three cryptographers and linguists were Peter Ericsson, Denis Oswald and myself. Together, we were the four founder members of the Testery. The Testery was actually a military army section – we were soon issued with our uniform and became Intelligence Corps, because there had been no time to lay on the usual training. As time went on there were more recruits, and we had a mixture of army personnel and civilians in the Testery.

A little later, two support staff joined us. They were Staff Sergeant 'Tubby' Roots and Lance Corporal Jim Walford. They were the Lorenz wheelsetters, and their job was to find the starting positions of each of the twelve wheels on Lorenz. Once they worked out the wheel patterns, they would prepare the materials for us to break. They did an excellent job, right through to the end of the war. Initially, there were not many people working at Bletchley when I first arrived there. Since we were a small team, we started in the Mansion, but a few months later we moved out and lodged in Hut 15A, situated at the end of tennis court and close to Huts 3 and 6.

Peter Ericsson and I were both 20 years old and seemed to do everything the same: we were made lieutenants on the same day, promoted to captains on the same day, became shift leaders on the same day, and we performed with equal success in breaking Lorenz.

Denis Oswald was about 30 years old. He must have been made a major somewhere else before he came to Bletchley Park. He was a pipe smoker, always very well groomed and was very different from Peter and me. He was the kind of man who is immensely methodical and when he started work in the morning he would have all his pencils sharpened and neatly in a row. He was very carefully turned out, his hair smoothed down and not a hair out of place; whereas Peter was much more casual and off-the-cuff, with a quite different nature. I was somewhere in the middle; not quite as dashing as Peter, but not as method-bound as Denis.

THE FIRST ASSIGNMENT: DOUBLE PLAYFAIR

Before working on the breaking of Lorenz, our first job was the break-ing of a cipher system used by the German Military Police, called Double Playfair. This was a relatively simple cipher system which had probably had been in use since the nineteenth century. It consisted of two square boxes in which the letters of the alphabet were organised at random, leaving out the letter 'Q'. The letters were organised in the first box in a random way and then organised in a different way in the second box. The message was enciphered in pairs of letters, according to special rules. The contents were hardly fascinating, unlike Lorenz, which we worked on from mid 1942 and was the most complex and secure system and, thus, the most challenging to work on.

Having broken one of the day's messages, the cryptographer had then to reconstruct the two boxes for that day so that all the other messages could be deciphered. I was rather slow on Double Playfair in the beginning, as anybody might be. Tester must have been quite worried as to whether I would make the grade. However, suddenly the penny dropped and within a few days I gained full confidence in my ability to deal with it. I had a good grasp of German, which is what was really needed for this kind of work. Once I had settled down, I managed to break one message, including working out the boxes, in twenty-one minutes – much faster than anyone else. This proved very important for me because I was keen to be considered when the need arose for people to work on Lorenz (the handful that were selected came mostly from this early stage of the Testery).

Double Playfair was apparently of no great importance. A typical message might run: 'Sgt. Schulz has been transferred from Inf. Div. 42 in Augsburg to Inf. Div. 36 in Munich'. This might appear to be of little interest, except possibly to Mrs Schulz. In reality, it did give us an indication of where these two infantry divisions were located, and this all helped in building up what is known as the 'order of battle' of the enemy.

The word used for 'sent' was '*inmarschgesetzt*' in German; the nearest equivalent in English would be 'set in motion', and it evoked a picture of a toy solider being wound up and let loose to walk. As such, the messages looked to be low grade. However, the messages often mentioned the army unit which the person was being sent to join and this helped in the process of building up or confirming the other side's troop positions. For this reason, the information had considerable importance.

Following Bill Tutte's amazing achievement in breaking the Lorenz system in spring 1942, we were immediately switched from Double Playfair to the daily breaking of Lorenz, the new twelve-wheel cipher system. The Testery was now where the real message breaking took place. Later on, the team would break over 90 per cent of the highest-level messages from the German Army High Command, including messages signed by Adolf Hitler himself.

About six years ago, I realised that I was the last survivor in Britain of the nine cryptographers who had worked on Lorenz in the Testery. Professor Jack Copeland told me that I was the last key person with first-hand experience of having been involved during this important period. If I concentrate, I can still remember the whole vivid picture of the Lorenz activities in my head.

It is worth recalling just what Hitler achieved in 1940–41: he conquered and took over France, Belgium, Austria, Holland, Poland, Czechoslovakia, some of the Baltic states and some of the Balkan states, as well as almost the whole of Europe, except Britain and a couple of neutrals such as Switzerland and Sweden. In 1940, Hitler must have been contemplating his plans for this, saw that his armies would be busily engaged and drew the conclusion that his generals needed a new cipher system in order to keep their communications secure from the enemy.

Many people have heard of or seen the film *Enigma* (made in 2001, starring Dougray Scott and Kate Winslett) and know about Alan Turing. So far, in my experience, most people have never heard of Lorenz or Bill Tutte. Lorenz decrypts provided vital information that changed the course of the war in Europe at critical junctures, such as the Battle of Kursk. Messages broken by the team in the Testery enabled the British government to warn Soviet leaders in 1943 about a major German offensive planned at Kursk that summer. The Soviet Army's repulse of the attack in the Battle of Kursk was a turning point of the war.

Lorenz decrypts also provided vital information for the operations both before and after D-Day. In particular, the Lorenz codebreakers helped to set the stage for D-Day by establishing, in the weeks before June 1944, that Hitler and his commanders expected an Allied invasion along the French coast at Calais, preceded by a feint at Normandy. The Germans were caught off guard by the full assault at Normandy.

HOW WE LIVED AT BLETCHLEY PARK

Bletchley in 1941 was a modest, small town with, as the wit said, a lot to be modest about. It owed its development to the London, Midland & Scottish Railway, being the first main stop outside London on the route to Birmingham and the north-west. People changed trains at Bletchley to get to Oxford or Cambridge, which were roughly equidistant from it. Of course, a fair number of rail workers lived in Bletchley, including my landlord Mr Wells.

When I joined Bletchley Park in 1941, it was estimated that less than 1,000 people worked at the Park (I was told about 700). Towards the end of the war, it was estimated there were 9,000–10,000 people involved in its activities, possibly more, excluding out-station workers. (Official figures indicate around 9,000 worked at Bletchley Park at its peak.) I was a fairly early resident and so was billeted in Bletchley itself and had a daily thirty-minute walk into and back from Bletchley Park along the length of the high street, with its mixture of small houses and small shops. I was fortunate to be given a billet with a working-class family in Fenny Stratford, a suburb. I used to do that walk regularly, there and back in the evening or whenever. I lived at No. 67 and the street was called Napier Street, after a Victorian general.

My wife Mei and I paid a visit to see how the billet looked seventy years later; it was after I gave my talk at Turing's 100th birthday event at Bletchley Park on 30 June 2012. The street was still there, as were the houses. Everywhere looked the same, although many of them had been improved upon, including No. 67. Basically, it was a tiny house with four rooms: two reception rooms downstairs and two double bedrooms upstairs. I had one double bedroom and one reception room, so I had half of the whole house. The toilet was in the backyard, which was pretty awkward.

The family who billeted me were very hospitable. The father worked on the railway, as so many people did in Bletchley. He had a son, Jack, in the army, a young daughter, Marjorie, and his wife Mrs Wells was a 50-year-old housewife. I have no doubt that the income which came to them from my being billeted there was useful, though it wouldn't have been very generous.

As an officer, I had quite a good income and very few costs. I spent the entire four years of my time working at Bletchley Park there. This was one example, out of many, of how the different social classes were thrown together during the war and came to have much more contact than they would have had in peacetime. I had, on some of my shifts, to get up and make my way to the Park early. Luckily, I did not need to disturb the family because Mr Wells himself was mostly on early call and got up at roughly the same time as I did. It was a very harmonious relationship with them and lasted pretty well for the four years.

When I was at the billet I used to eat with the family, but of course many items of food, such as butter, sugar, milk, etc., were rationed, so I had to give up my ration book to Mrs Wells. The rest of my meals I had up at the Park in the canteen. These, in the same way, were pretty basic. We were, in fact, very lucky to have as much food as we did, especially in 1941 when the U-boats were wreaking great destruction on our merchant shipping. However, once Turing had broken the naval Enigma the situation improved and you could see the improvement in people's daily lives. Fewer ships were sunk, and more food came in.

Bletchley consisted mainly of a long high street ending near the station with some pockets of better housing on one side and many two-storey terrace houses where, even in their main rooms, it would be difficult to swing the proverbial cat. It was quiet, perhaps dull even, but worthy. It offered relatively little in the way of entertainment and the more with-it, younger Bletchley Park people lived for the day they could flee to London and the social whirl, even if only for twenty-four hours.

As the war went on, Bletchley Park developed and took on larger numbers of Auxiliary Territorial Service (ATS), WAAFs and Wrens. As they were all young ladies they lodged outside Bletchley, often in stately homes in an area of 10 miles around the town, or else in homes in the villages. As a consequence, these members of the staff had to be bussed in to start their shifts at the Park and then bussed back again at the end of their day.

In our unit, Peter Edgerley and Peter Hilton both came to the Testery a year later than me. They were given billets outside Bletchley, near Bedford. Many of them had to take one of the Bletchley Park coaches in and out each day. There were many pick-up and drop-off points and it was very well organised.

Entertainment at Bletchley was limited. There was a cinema in the town which changed its programme once a week. There were few shops or cafes. Up at the Park, there were a number of clubs such as the cheese club, drama club, film club and so on, but I was usually too tired at the end of a shift to go on to a chess club or the dramatic society and usually made my way home. Very occasionally, the Wrens would hold a dance at the country house in which they were billeted and these were special occasions, much enjoyed. But they might only happen twice a year or perhaps three times – not very often. Special transport was laid on and these were well attended, the more so for their rarity.

In the office, everyone just put their heads down and got on with their work, with not much chatting, but occasionally we would have a chat when we took a break for a few minutes. Peter Hilton sometimes had a story to tell us about his landlady – the splendid Mrs Butler. Mrs Butler came out with wonderful malapropisms – 'the Pope and all his cardigans' (cardinals) – and mangled words – 'interlollopers' (interlopers). Each new Butlerism was eagerly awaited by Peter's colleagues. He relayed them, however, with no hint of malice or condescension – a typical touch of his kindliness. He had a great sense of humour.

I enjoyed the work itself. I never got bored with breaking messages and never lost the thrill of getting the break-in. I was billeted thirty minutes' walk away from Bletchley Park – quite close to the Park compared to the thousands of people who lived much further away. I bought myself a good radio which I installed in my reception room, and after work, some of the time, I used to listen to classical music and the news in the evening. My love of such music really dates from that time.

Anyone who opted to spend their evening in the town or at Bletchley Park was obliged to take the midnight coach and get to bed around 1 a.m., needing to take an 8 a.m. coach the next day to be in by 9.a.m. There was no other bus before midnight because of the shortage of petrol. Social activity was a good deal blunted by this situation. Romance and Bletchley Park were, we suspect, not easily compatible; people simply lived too far away from each other and transport was very limited. But some people did get together, had affairs and even got married.

Another interesting juxtaposition arose from the billeting of people with a professional or semi-professional background in the homes of industrial workers. It was not uncommon for one class to have contact at the workplace with the other, but it was highly unusual in those days for the two classes to live side by side in this way – at a time when the class divide was a great deal wider than it is today. War, and in particular the ration book, was a great leveller:

everyone lived quite the same, but often in a harmonious way with other social groups.

While there was nobody in the town who knew just what went on at the Park (the rumour ran that it was Littlewoods Pools up there), there were many in the Park itself who had no concrete – or even vague – idea of what really happened there. The basis was 'need to know' – you were told as much or as little as your seniors felt was necessary.

At the station end of the High Street and 300 yards up a hill was the small road leading to the security gates at the entrance to Bletchley Park, set in a high security fence. It was a striking contrast between the town itself, which was the essence of everyday humdrumness, and Bletchley Park, with its dramatic work going on twenty-four hours a day, often affecting crucial decisions in the conduct of the war and – not the least remarkable aspect of the work there – the development of the first ever electronic computer.

6

HITLER'S TOP-SECRET CODE: LORENZ (TUNNY)

WHAT WAS LORENZ?

Lorenz was what the Germans called it originally. Tunny was a code name given by Bletchley Park. We simply called it Fish.

The Germans' Lorenz was a new enciphering machine, more secure and more complex than Enigma, which was ordered by Adolf Hitler himself in 1940 and built by the Lorenz Electrical Company, based in Berlin. The Lorenz Company produced a number of typewriters and telegraph sets, including a teleprinter which enciphered messages based on the teleprinter code. The earlier model of Lorenz was called SZ40 and a later model was called SZ42. 'SZ' stands for '*Schlüsselzusatz*', which means 'special attachment', so called because the SZ machines were attachments to the standard teleprinters.

This specially designed attachment was a much advanced cipher system and more secure in comparison to earlier machines. The German Army started to use the SZ in the second half of 1940 and from mid 1942 on it was used for communication between the German Army High Command in Berlin and Army Group High Commands across Europe. Unlike Enigma, which had three wheels, the Lorenz had twelve wheels and was the highest form of technology at that time. It was the 'the secret writer' of which Hitler dreamed. The Lorenz SZ40/42 was a wonderful machine: it should never, ever have been broken.

In mid 1940, the first Lorenz link went into operation on wireless telegraphy. The messages were picked up by the British 'Y' wireless intercept station and then sent to Bletchley for decrypting. The SZ began to be used by the German Army, and the first link we called Fish. Fish referred to encrypted German links from the teleprinter traffic. Bletchley Park gave each link in this network a different fish code name, such as Bream, Herring, Jellyfish and so on, and eventually there were up to twenty-six Fish links.

The Lorenz SZ40/42 enciphered teleprinter traffic, which used a five-bit Baudot code, each letter being built up from electrical impulses, which could be positive or negative. We used dot (•) as negative and x for positive. Thus, letter A was shown as x x • • •, letter B was shown as x • •x x, and so on.

They were radio messages produced by teleprinters, and there were two similar types of these cipher machines in use by the Germans: the Lorenz *Schlüsselzusatz* SZ40/42 and Siemens T52, which the Germans called *Geheimschreiber* ('secret writer'). The two systems were not compatible with each other. Bletchley Park only dealt with Lorenz SZ40/42 – the traffic we broke was the most important top-level secret code in the Fish links.

WHY WAS LORENZ SO IMPORTANT?

At its peak in 1944, towards the end of the war, Lorenz decrypts provided intelligence of unprecedented quality, containing the most top-level secrets. Tens of thousands of Tunny messages were intercepted by the British and broken at Bletchley Park by my fellow codebreakers, teammates and me in the Testery section.

Lorenz carried only the highest levels of top-secret intelligence: messages passed primarily from the German Army Headquarters in Berlin and the Army Group High Commands to the top generals and field marshals on all the main battle fronts in Europe, and the army groups' five key links on the main battle fronts. They went almost exclusively to the heads of the huge armies. We can get some idea of Lorenz's significance if we consider the people who signed the messages. They included:

Field Marshal Keitel (head of the German Army)
Field Marshal Jodl (chief of staff)
General Warlimont (Western Front, deputy to Jodl)
General von Rundstedt (Western Front)
General Model (Western Front)
General von Kluge (Western Front, head of all armies in France after D-Day)
General Field Marshal von Weichs (Russian Front)
Field Marshal von Manstein (Russian Front)
Field Marshal Rommel (North Africa, later Commander Northern France)
Field Marshal Kesselring (Western Front, Italian Peninsula)
Adolf Hitler (starting in early 1944)

From this you can see the importance of the traffic that we broke at Bletchley Park; most of the messages came from these men. They were a handful of extremely capable and aggressive members of the German Army High Command during the Second World War.

Later on, quite a number of messages were signed by Hitler himself. I recall breaking some of them myself, signed simply 'Adolf. Hitler. Fuehrer'. It was a real thrill when I saw these messages before they were even received by the German High Command in the field.

The breaking of Lorenz made vital contributions to the successful operation of the war and enabled the Allies to win the war early. General Eisenhower commented after the war that Bletchley decrypts shortened the war by at least two years. If the D-Day landings had failed, it would have taken at least two years to prepare another major assault and it would have lost tens of millions of lives.

THE LORENZ NETWORK: FIVE MAIN LORENZ LINKS

The Testery worked with a particular focus on the five most important links in Europe. From the middle of 1942 onwards, we broke messages from each of these five main links:

Russian Front North
Russian Front Central
Russian Front South
Western Front
Italian Peninsula

The Russian Fronts were sometimes referred to as the Eastern Fronts. There were two major central exchanges for Lorenz traffic: the western links went into Berlin and the eastern links with Russia went into Königsberg in eastern Germany. We called the link from headquarters to Army Group G the 'West Front'.

The Lorenz began with a single link, but spread rapidly throughout Europe as the German Army top brass came to value it highly. It was easier to use and much more secure than Enigma. The strategic value of the Lorenz information was immense. One long message alone, for instance, gave the whole disposition of the units within the army groups on the Eastern Front and, within each army, the divisions, panzer divisions and other specialised units in each army.

From Lorenz decrypts, a vast mass of messages was read, enabling us to learn a great deal about the enemy's strategic thinking, planning and decision-making. Messages were broken to help in many crucial situations – such as the critical Battle of Kursk in 1943, the clearing of the Italian Peninsula in 1944 and the months before and after D-Day. The war cost at least 55 million lives between 1939 and 1945, so shortening it by two years could have saved up to 20 million lives.

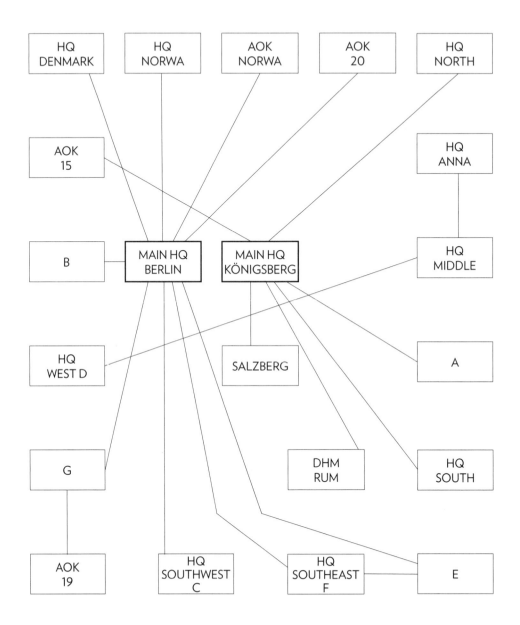

Links showing the reach of Lorenz-encrypted messages between 1942 and 1945. Note: the individual letters are the headquarters of the Army Group concerned

7

HOW LORENZ WAS DIFFERENT FROM ENIGMA

During the Second World War there were two major high-grade cipher systems worked on at Bletchley Park: Enigma and the Lorenz (Tunny). Both systems were broken and a large proportion of the messages deciphered at Bletchley Park. The work on Enigma became known to the public much earlier than Lorenz. The story of Enigma is quite well known, given that it has received relatively wide coverage on television and radio and it has also been the subject of films and books. In contrast, there is little public awareness of Bletchley Park's attack on Lorenz, nor even of the existence of Lorenz itself.

In many respects, the breaking of Lorenz is a missing piece of history, and, to a large extent, this is because Lorenz was only declassified in 2002, in comparison to Enigma which was declassified in the 1970s. Thus Lorenz was kept secret for approximately sixty years after the war.

COMPARISON OF THE TWO MACHINES

Enigma: Three-Wheel Cipher Machine
  Declassified in the 1970s.
  Used from 1923 onwards, for air, land and sea traffic.
  Well known through print, TV and film.
  Naval Enigma broken by Alan Turing in June 1941.
  Enigma decrypts helped Britain not to lose the war in 1941.

Lorenz: Twelve-Wheel Cipher Machine

Declassified only in 2002.

Used from 1940 onwards by the German Army.

Used by Hitler, his High Command and top generals.

More advanced, complex, faster and more secure than Enigma.

Bill Tutte broke Lorenz system in spring 1942 (without ever having seen the machine).

Lorenz decrypts helped shorten the Second World War in Europe.

Enigma was used on lower-level messages from the field, in the air and at sea. Alan Turing broke the Enigma code as used by the German Navy. His work on Enigma is widely remembered for its significance in tackling the threat from German U-boats during the Battle of the Atlantic in the middle of 1941, as a result of which Britain was saved.

Lorenz was used for transmitting the highest grade of intelligence messages at the top level. Lorenz decrypts made a major contribution to winning the war. Bill Tutte's breaking of the Lorenz system without having ever seen the machine was a phenomenal achievement, but many people have never heard of him.

Enigma and Lorenz were two very different cipher systems and had very little in common. Enigma, with its three wheels, created messages using the twenty-six-letter alphabet. It could send out a code in 150 million, million different start positions. The Lorenz SZ40/42, however, was much more sophisticated, with twelve wheels and 501 pins. Enciphered messages sent by teleprinter used 5-bit punched paper tape. Thus, the Lorenz could send out a code with around 1.6 quadrillion different start positions. Arguably, Lorenz was even more significant and far more complex than Enigma. It was a miracle that Bill Tutte was able to break the Lorenz system with very little to go on.

Lorenz was used for sending teleprinter messages, where a message often contained thousands of 'places' (characters, letters or spaces), whereas Enigma messages often contained fewer than 300. Lorenz used twelve wheels to produce the key sequence, one key letter for each of the plain message letters. These wheels, called pin wheels, are completely different from the wheels of the Enigma machine.

The wheel settings were changed every day by the Germans, although they were changed less frequently in the early stages of the war. From January 1944, the wheel patterns changed every single day, on the five major links. Lorenz had more wheels than Enigma so the pattern was quite different and more complex. The Lorenz pattern could be changed very easily and frequently. The code-breakers in the Testery had to break the message daily by hand, in order to find out all the patterns and wheel settings at the time. Once the message was broken, we could break the rest of the traffic for that day.

Lorenz produced a system that was much easier to use than Enigma. Compared with Enigma, the Lorenz was much more efficient. Lorenz needed only one operator at each end, while Enigma called for three people at each end – one to prepare the message, one to convert it into Morse code and the third to transmit it over the air. With Lorenz, the operator simply typed in the message on the keyboard and the machine automatically enciphered it and sent it off.

It can be imagined how confident the Germans must have been in something as complex as Lorenz. They had reason to be: the number of letters before a setting would be repeated was enormous, because the number of combinations generated by ten of the twelve wheels was a prime number and their combined multiplication reached a staggering sum. As a result, the German Army entrusted their most important communications not to Enigma but to Lorenz.

I was told by Oliver Lawn, one of the top cryptographers who worked on Enigma himself, that the cryptographer could cipher text on Enigma up to twelve places and didn't even need to know German. I find it difficult to class all the machine work on the Enigma as that kind of cryptography, because of the dependence on the machine. But for Lorenz, around fifty places of cipher text had to be broken to establish the wheel patterns of the day, and for individual messages thereafter twenty or so places had to be broken to fix the start points on each of the twelve wheels.

Even if one had good German, it was still very challenging. If I were to send you a message and encrypt it, I would probably choose letter substitution – for instance, A will be X, B will be Y, C will be Z and so on. We would agree the system beforehand. This would be *one* level of encryption. Lorenz had not one, not two, but *three* levels of encryption.

In the early years of the Second World War, the Germans already had great confidence in their Enigma enciphering system, which Bletchley Park nonetheless had broken. A fourth wheel was later added, but even so Turing managed to break the naval Enigma in June 1941. He also invented the Bombe machines to greatly speed up the breaking process on Enigma – but not on Lorenz.

Turing played a vital role in deciphering the messages encrypted on the naval Enigma. He was already quite well known when I first went to Bletchley Park in autumn 1941. A reconstruction of a Turing-Welchman Bombe machine can today be seen in action at Bletchley Park where one of the volunteer guides, Jean Valentine, who was a Bombe operator during the war, is one of a handful of operators who demonstrate the machine to visitors.

I used to see Alan Turing from time to time at the Park: a man of medium height, 29 at that time, dressed in a sports jacket and rather baggy grey trousers (a bit like mine). He would walk along the corridor in one of the huts with his gaze averted from other people, looking at the bottom of the wall and flicking the wall with his fingers. While not very comfortable in company and certainly a shy man, he was on very good terms and sociable with other mathematicians of his kind. You would never guess that this was the most influential man in Europe at that particular time. He was no hero figure, but he made an enormous difference and saved Britain from a Nazi dark age.

Enigma was invented in Germany after the First World War in 1923. A number of models were produced and it was improved over the years. Before Turing broke the naval Enigma, there were people from other countries who tried to break the system. The Polish initially broke into it in the 1930s; at that time, the Enigma machine was not a great secret – you could even buy one on the open market in the post office. The German military adopted it for their use during the early years of the war. However, the methods devised by the Poles to break into Enigma were not very effective for the circumstances of the Second World War.

From 1939 onwards, the breaking of Enigma was taken up by Bletchley Park. Alan Turing and his team, Dilly Knox, Hugh Alexander, Gordon Welchman and perhaps others, all worked on it. Dilly made a substantial contribution to the breaking of Enigma by providing vital information to Turing, and his team also made a number of visits to talk with the Poles about their techniques for breaking Enigma.

Codebreaker Mavis Batey lays out clearly who did what in her book, *Dilly: The Man Who Broke Enigmas* (Dialogue, 2010). She herself achieved a remarkable success; she worked on Enigma as used by the Italian Navy, and one evening, while her colleagues were at dinner, she managed to break the system. She was only 19 at the time. As a result, the British were able to read the Italian traffic before the Battle of Matapan in early 1941, which was of crucial importance. The British Royal Navy defeated the Italian Navy comprehensively at the cape off the south-west coast of Greece. The Italian fleet never emerged from port for the rest of the war. This was another example of how the work at Bletchley Park exercised a major influence on the course of the war.

Turing's breaking of the naval Enigma had not only saved Britain from defeat at the hands of the Nazis, but also helped save Britain in 1941. In 1940–41, the great threat came from Hitler's U-boats, which were sinking large numbers of merchant ships bringing food and war supplies to Britain. By mid 1941, the British were losing merchant shipping with average losses of 282,000 tonnes monthly. The sinking of ships with food and war materials reached an appalling level. Britain could only have lasted a few months more before it was starved out by the German U-boats and would have lost the war.

I once talked with someone who had sailed in a convoy early in 1941. He had been a brave man in the SAS. He said, 'We left port with twenty-one ships and arrived in Britain with just eleven.' The U-boats had sunk nearly half the whole convoy, and this was happening time and time again in the Atlantic. After Turing's achievement, there was a massive decline in the number of ships sunk. The losses dropped to 120,000 tonnes monthly and by November even lower, to 62,000 tonnes.

In early 1942, the Germans added a fourth wheel to the Enigma machines used in the U-boats. This made it much more difficult, as we could no longer decipher messages: sinkings shot up again and Britain was once more faced with the grave risk of starvation and defeat at the hands of a by now much larger force of U-boats. Sonar and the Liberator bombers that patrolled the oceans offered no salvation at all at this perilous time. It was only when we were again able to break naval Enigma that the sinkings dropped to a lower level – bad enough, but supportable. This was due to the bravery of two navy men – Fasson and Grazier – who boarded *U-559* when it was damaged by gunfire from a British destroyer and abandoned by its crew. The two men rescued the logbooks for the new four-wheel system and handed them to the third member of their party – Tommy Brown, who was only 16 and worked in the NAAFI. They were rushed to Bletchley Park and after brilliant work by Turing's team it was once again possible to decipher naval Enigma messages.

Turing was already well known for his work on Enigma, and he also became a well-known and rather eccentric figure at Bletchley Park. He suffered from hay fever in the spring and could often be seen riding his bicycle with his gas mask on as he made his way to the Park. He also didn't like the pollution produced by motor cars and again would often wear his gas mask to filter out the fumes. He used to keep his coffee cup on a chain so that nobody else could use it.

Another story well known at the Park was that Turing was very interested in learning how to shoot either a rifle or a pistol, and for this purpose he joined the Home Guard. For a number of months he turned up at all the drills, but after a while his attendance began to drop off as he became busier and busier at Bletchley. He was reprimanded from time to time by the colonel in charge of the Home Guard because of his poor attendance rate.

He was finally summoned to a meeting to give an account of himself. He explained his situation, but the colonel would take no notice.

He said to Turing, 'This is now very serious. You remember when you joined the Home Guard, you signed a form saying you accepted King's regulations?'

Turing queried this, saying, 'Did I?'

'Yes, of course you did,' replied the colonel.

'I don't remember that,' Turing answered.

The colonel furiously insisted on producing the actual form Turing had signed. 'There!'

However, at the question 'you recognise that in signing this form you are accepting King's regulations', Turing had written 'No'. Nobody had spotted this at the time, because no recruit ever wrote 'No' at this point. The colonel dismissed Turing and told him never to darken his door again.

This was typical of Turing's logical approach to things. Bill Tutte and Alan Turing were both great mathematicians. Turing is most well known to the public, who generally believe that he was the leading mathematical codebreaker at Bletchley Park. In my view, Tutte had an even more difficult job in breaking Lorenz, without ever seeing the machine.

8

BILL TUTTE BREAKS THE LORENZ SYSTEM

Bill Tutte was born into a family of modest means, the only child of a gardener in Newmarket, Suffolk. From his early days he was very keen to study. He had to travel 12 miles to go to school every day. He won academic prizes in every subject. He then went on to Trinity College, Cambridge, where he took a degree in chemistry and mathematics. When he was a student there, still only 18 years old, he became the first to solve the famous old problem of 'Squaring the Square' (filling a square with other small squares, all of different sizes, to make up the total space).

In 1941, at the height of the Second World War, Bletchley Park needed talented mathematicians urgently and his tutor, Patrick Duff, recommended him to the Park. Tutte had originally been interviewed by Alan Turing for work at Bletchley Park, but he was rejected. Luckily, he was interviewed again by Colonel Tiltman, who saw his potential and accepted him. He joined the Research Section. This team was made up of high-flyers who were available to help other units at Bletchley Park with particularly difficult problems.

I was also interviewed by Colonel Tiltman shortly after I arrived at Bletchley Park as a civilian in autumn 1941. I was delighted he accepted me and thought I was a suitable person to work on Lorenz. I can still remember the interview I had with him. He wore his full uniform, complete with red tabs, and it was a rather intimidating encounter. I was half-terrified by the red tabs of a staff colonel. He was about 45 years old, with a moustache. He must have realised what kind of staff he needed to deal with this important new cipher system, and he repeatedly emphasised the importance of the work carried out at Bletchley Park and the absolute silence about it which had to be preserved. I took this very much to heart: both my parents died in the 1970s without knowing anything of the work I had been engaged in during my four years at Bletchley Park. Afterwards, I saw Colonel Tiltman often in the Park; he actually had a very positive and friendly attitude.

As early as 1940, when British radio operators began to intercept transmissions in enciphered teleprinter code, they realised they were listening to a new kind of 'music'. It became clear that the Germans had developed a number of different cipher machines for use in conjunction with the teleprinter equipment. Bletchley Park gave the ciphers code names corresponding to species of fish, hence Lorenz's code name Tunny.

A critical event occurred on 30 August 1941. The German Army Radio Operator A in Athens sent a message to his colleague, Operator B in Salzburg, Austria. Operator B was not satisfied with the transmission and asked Operator A to send it again. He did so, but he made two catastrophic errors: first, he did not change the wheel settings, putting his Lorenz SZ40/42 back to exactly the same wheel start positions as had been used on the previous failed transmission; second, when he sent it the second time, he compounded his error by abbreviating some German words, which he hadn't done the first time.

The whole message was 4,000 places (characters) long, and these slight changes made a shift of four places to the left. This encoding of two close, but slightly different, forms of a message with slightly different encoding patterns was called a 'depth' and was incredibly valuable to us cryptographers. Depths were easier for cryptographers to break than single messages as the two messages could be compared.

The offending messages were received and the job was passed to Colonel John Tiltman, the most experienced cryptographer in the British Army and quite possibly on the British side. The process is described below.

Unlike Enigma, Lorenz messages tended to be much longer, running into many thousands of places. Enigma messages were usually less than 300 places in length. Using the Lorenz system to encode a message was easier since a single operator could just type the message on the teleprinter keyboard and the stream of letters would be automatically encoded and transmitted. The Enigma, by contrast, required the operator to read the message and type the letters on the Enigma keyboard and a second person would then read the corresponding letters that were illuminated and then transmit the message by Morse code, which was more time consuming. Similarly, when receiving Enigma messages the process was reversed, but with Lorenz the code was automatically received, decoded and printed onto paper by the machine itself, making the transmission and reception of messages much faster, secure and the most up to date.

HOW DID BILL TUTTE BREAK THE LORENZ SYSTEM WITHOUT EVER SEEING THE MACHINE?

The two messages between Athens and Salzburg were intercepted by the British and sent to Bletchley Park, where the initial work on the system was carried out by the Research Section. The enciphered messages were given to Colonel Tiltman. He worked on the messages for ten days and an early break was made – each had the same text with minor differences and he was able to decipher the two messages by adding them together to make a 'key'. He knew they were a 'depth' because they contained the same number of letters, indicating that they had been enciphered in exactly the same way, using the same start positions on each of the twelve wheels. He could then try adding a frequently used expression to the key and it would produce a reasonable piece of German when he found the right place in the message.

The Germans were very careless in their use of Lorenz, especially during its early days of operation. Lorenz should have been much harder to break than it was, but they enciphered and transmitted two, three or even more messages on the same wheel settings. Any two of these made a depth.

However, Colonel Tiltman was unable to work out how the Lorenz cipher system itself worked. Even though this 4,000-character-long material was now available, it still needed a genius to see its possibilities and to break the system.

This genius was Bill Tutte. When Tiltman failed to work out the system, the job was passed on to the 24-year-old mathematics graduate. He started working out how the Lorenz code wheels worked by writing out squares on paper and looking for patterns within the number sequence, using mathematics and structural logic. He established early on a method of working out the five chi wheel patterns from scratch on a single message of 4,000 characters (as opposed to a depth) which then allowed the five psi wheels and two motor wheels to be worked out. This was a very important breakthrough and laid the basis for the later mechanised chi wheel breaking by the Colossus machine.

Working with a sample of intercepted messages, Tutte, by intellect and intuition alone, deduced that the Lorenz code was generated by a machine with a series of rotors. He noticed that the first of these had forty-one teeth and then went on to work out all twelve rotors correctly. The Lorenz machine was broken – how the twelve wheels worked, their lengths and their functions – everything worked out. His breaking of the system was an extraordinary achievement.

I was working in the same office as Bill Tutte when he was breaking the Lorenz system in spring 1942 and saw at first hand his endless patience and persistence. For all that time, I saw him staring into the middle distance for extended periods, twiddling his pencil and making endless counts on reams of paper for nearly three months, and I used to wonder whether he was getting anything done – my goodness, he was! It was painstaking work and an extraordinary feat of the mind, to break something which used triple encryption. His concentration paid off handsomely in this, the most difficult system to break in the history of cryptography.

Tutte himself was rather a reserved person, modest and likeable, but not one for much social chat. We were on good terms but did not talk a great deal with each other. We were like two Native Americans from different tribes, who were friendly but did not speak each other's language; he was a mathematician and I was a linguist/codebreaker. I have a great deal of admiration for Tutte and for what he achieved, and feel he has been greatly undervalued.

The first time Tutte saw the Lorenz SZ40/42 cipher machine was when he went to Germany after the war. He was shown it by a German intelligence officer who explained how complex the machine was. Tutte had to stand there shaking his head and saying things like 'no one is ever going to break that then'. He was not allowed to reveal that he himself had broken it.

Tutte's work not only provided the tools for the cryptographers to break Lorenz traffic, but also gave Tommy Flowers the opportunity to design and build the Colossus, the world's first programmable digital computer, which was used to assist the Testery department's hand breaking of the chi wheel positions. However, the remaining psi and motor wheels were still hand broken by the Testery. Tutte's achievement was later described as one of the greatest intellectual feats of the war and has in fact been called by one commentator, 'the outstanding mental feat of the last century'.

9

THE TESTERY BREAKS THE LORENZ CODE BY HAND

CHURCHILL ORDERS, 'ACTION THIS DAY!'

As the war progressed, the volume of messages rose. Britain's wartime prime minister, Winston Churchill, paid a visit to Bletchley Park in September 1941. A month later, four of most senior codebreakers at Bletchley Park, Alan Turing, Gordon Welchman, Hugh Alexander and Stuart Milner-Barry, wrote to Churchill directly, saying that Bletchley urgently needed to recruit more staff. Churchill immediately granted permission and replied famously, 'Action this day!' and added to his reply, 'Make sure they have all they want on extreme priority and report to me that this has been done.' Indeed, this came at a good time for the Testery, as we expanded substantially over the next eighteen months. Churchill was never in any doubt about the importance of what we were doing at Bletchley Park.

HOW WE WERE ORGANISED AS A TEAM

Once Bill Tutte had broken the system, he had opened the door for us cryptographers in the Testery to work on the Lorenz traffic. From 1 July 1942 onwards, we switched from Double Playfair to working on the daily breaking of Lorenz. Until the end of the war, the Testery remained the only team working on breaking Lorenz by hand.

When I started in the Testery in 1941, the unit numbered only eight or nine persons. Over the next few years, however, the Lorenz work advanced enough to require more cryptographers and support staff and the team grew steadily. By the end of the war, the Testery had extended to a total staff of 118, including twenty-four ATS girls, nine cryptanalysts and all kinds of support staff, all organised in three shifts working round the clock. The Testery was a small team in relation to the quantity and quality of deciphered material produced.

There were three main shift leaders, of which I was one; the other two were Peter Ericsson and Victor Masters. Three of us – the original cryptographers – were sort of superstars; we played the major role, working on the daily breaking of Lorenz right from the start until the end of the war. Without our work, nothing could go forwards. We greatly enjoyed our work, because we kept up such high levels of success in breaking traffic. It was a very exciting period and we worked extremely hard with great enthusiasm to meet the daily challenge of messages.

We had started breaking messages purely by hand for the first twelve months, without any help from machines. The messages broken amounted to 1.5 million characters of cipher text during this phase of hand breaking. Once it became possible to break depth messages, we were very busy. We were breaking Lorenz messages manually, through all seven stages. The activities included working out the patterns on each of the twelve wheels.

A year later, the 'Newmanry' was set up with machines that would help the Testery to speed up one stage of the breaking process: determining the chi wheel settings.

The Testery was only a small unit at first, but was sufficient to break the relatively limited amount of traffic intercepted in the early stages of the war. At that time, we – the three original senior cryptographers – had created very special positions in the early stages of the attack on Lorenz. We established successful methods for breaking around fifty consecutive places of cipher text, we would then work out again by hand all three sets of wheel patterns – chi wheels, psi wheels and motor wheels – thus allowing most of the day's traffic to be deciphered. After the codebreakers had done their work, then the wheelsetters took over and established the start points of each of the twelve wheels. There were some twenty wheelsetters, and support staff did the remaining stages of their important work.

The codebreakers had been augmented steadily up to nine by mid 1944. Naturally, the latecomers were much slower than the three of us original cryptographers and more restricted in terms of their ability to break messages quickly. It was unfortunate that the change had taken place because it was tougher for them to get used to the new system when they had not had the experience of the old one. Some of them were not as fluent in German either. Thus, John Christie, on my shift, struggled hard to break messages from time to time. It was very hard going for him and it must have been the same on the other two shifts. For Roy Jenkins, too, it was particularly frustrating. This is why the three original codebreakers probably did the majority of the message breaking.

In one sense, people's skill levels varied enormously. Peter Ericsson and I had a lot of experience, while others would fumble and stumble for hours with little or no result. This was, of course, nothing compared with the experiences of Bill Tutte as he struggled to break the Lorenz system or changes in the system, where frustration might last for days, weeks, even months. The patience and persistence he exercised was truly remarkable. Taken all in all, the Testery cryptographers did an astonishingly good job.

The security at Bletchley Park was extremely tight, which everybody respected. I never asked anyone else what they did and I certainly did not tell anyone else what I had worked on, not even my parents. It stayed that way, not only at Bletchley Park but also for nearly sixty years after the war. The first I heard about Lorenz after the war was when Professor Jack Copeland invited me to write a chapter for his book *Colossus* (OUP, 2006). His book was the first that mentioned Lorenz, the Testery and the people involved. I had forgotten about Bletchley Park for all those years. Suddenly, my recollections were sharp and clear, the result of spending my four solid years at Bletchley Park from 1941 to 1945.

Luckily, towards the end of the war in 1945, I kept a copy of the original list of personnel in the Testery, with the names of all 118 staff on it. If I had been caught at the time, I could have been in serious trouble, but it has been an invaluable document ever since. In recent years, I have been able to help people's relatives to identify their loved ones. It is also a vivid reminder of many of my colleagues from so many years ago. I gave a copy to Tom Colvill in 1995, who had been the general manager of the Testery. He was able to put me in contact with Ralph Tester, who became a good friend instead of a much-liked boss. We were in touch with each other for two years before he sadly died.

Most of us in the Testery were very young for such responsible work. Peter Hilton, who joined in December 1942, was only 19. I was getting on a bit because I was 20 when I joined the Intelligence Corps, the same as Peter Ericsson. Ralph Tester was certainly an older man by far, in his 40s, and Denis Oswald was positively venerable at around 30. He taught German at Uppingham before joining Bletchley Park. Peter Edgerley and Donald Michie were even younger at only 18 – they joined in early 1943. Donald Michie was a clever mathematician, who joined straight from school and performed well. He was moved into the Newmanry after a few months. The ATS girls were all under 24 during 1944, when most of them joined to cope with the sharp rise in the number of Lorenz messages. We were all away from family, billeted in or around Bletchley Park.

In the course of the four years I was there, the Testery moved house three times. At first, I worked in the Mansion, then after two months or so the Testery was moved to a temporary Hut 15a (near the end of the tennis court, which was not far from the Mansion). The Testery only had a few people then, in a good-sized room. I remember clearly, in early spring 1942, it was there that Tutte had his space in our room, where I saw him working on Lorenz. Later, by the end of 1943, once more huts had been constructed, the Testery moved again to Block F. We occupied a larger space, close to the Newmanry. The proximity to the Newmanry was due to needing to have close contact with the machine team to help the Testery with hand breaking.

The move to Block F was a prime example of how the management had to keep reacting to changes in the demands of the work. The rooms were very plain and simple. For instance, in our breakers' room, there was space for four to five people (but normally only two or three were in each shift), each with simple wooden desks and chairs, and at the end of the room for a large table for writing material – paper, pencils and erasers – and nothing much else. The messages to be broken were placed in a pile, including any left over from the previous shift.

There was a small kitchen area down the corridor where staff could make hot drinks with their own rationed tea. We could take a short break anytime we wanted for light relief from the intensive effort we had to put into the breaking of messages.

We ran a three-shift system from mid 1943 onwards; covering twenty-four hours a day, seven days a week. We all had one day off a week and we changed our shift every week. In the early stages, everyone worked on one shift and most of the people were engaged in the breaking process. As time went on and the sheer volume of decrypting grew, it became necessary to have an evening shift. A little later, as the wheels for more army groups were broken, a midnight shift was added so that there was round-the-clock machine deciphering going on.

Each team would work one week on days (9 a.m.–4 p.m.), one week on evenings (4 p.m.–12 p.m.) and one week on nights (12 p.m.–9 a.m.). While in the daytime the shift personnel could take any major problem to the management or senior codebreakers, this was not possible for the midnight shift or after 6 p.m. for the evening group. Shift leaders were appointed, of which I was one, with the duties falling largely to Captain Peter Ericsson, myself and Victor Masters (not a codebreaker). We would still participate in message breaking but also had the responsibility of keeping the decrypting process going smoothly over the whole shift.

Tester himself led the team extremely well; he had his own office next door to our breakers in Room 41. He was not a cryptographer but had a real job on his hands in running such a mixed bag of people in the Testery. We had army officers and other ranks, civilians, ATS girls in army uniform, codebreakers, wheelsetters, support staff and so on. I was an army officer and wore uniform most of the time. Tester himself usually wore uniform, as did Ericsson and Oswald.

Tester was very good at handling people; nobody was ever fired or transferred to another unit. They had all been picked well, from the right places, to do the right job, no time was wasted on unnecessary admin and all of us stayed until the end of the war. I can only speak for the Testery, but it was a model of efficiency, inspiration and good organisation, in which there was always a positive friendly spirit, much helped by the continual success day after day.

THE FOUR MAIN GROUPS IN THE TESTERY AFTER EXPANSION

1. The Three Senior Codebreakers and the Rest

Captain Jerry Roberts (shift leader, senior codebreaker and German linguist, 1941)
Captain Peter Ericsson (shift leader, senior codebreaker and German linguist, 1941)
Major Denis Oswald (senior codebreaker, German linguist, 1941)

The following staff joined the Testery from mid 1942 to 1944:

Mr Victor Masters (shift leader)
RSM Peter Benenson (codebreaker)
Mr Peter Edgerley (codebreaker)
Mr Peter Hilton (mathematician and codebreaker)
Mr John Christie (codebreaker)
Mr Jack Thompson (codebreaker)
Captain H. Dobbins (codebreaker)
Captain Roy Jenkins (codebreaker for three months, then wheelsetter)
Dr Max Newman (codebreaker for three months, left to set up the Newmanry)

Mr Jack Good (codebreaker for a couple of months, went to Newmanry)

Mr Donald Michie (mathematician and codebreaker, went to Newmanry)

Peter Ericsson and I were both main shift leaders and codebreakers at Room 41. We were breaking each day's traffic at the first stage by hand, in order to allow us to break the rest of the traffic on that day. We were almost like twin brothers and good friends, since we had so many similarities: we were both aged 20 when we joined and both very capable, except we were on different shifts. We were able to break messages more quickly than other codebreakers; because we understood German well, we could identify break-ins much faster. We also seemed to have a cryptographer's instinct for break-ins. After the war, I was transferred immediately by the Foreign Office to Europe to work with the War Crimes Investigation Unit, while Peter and many others at Bletchley Park had to wait for their new jobs. Sadly, we lost contact and I never saw or heard from Peter again.

Denis Oswald, the third original member, was an excellent linguist and message breaker. A pipe smoker aged 30ish, he conveyed the impression of great calm. He worked well but more slowly; he was very methodical, and when breaking he tended to use a laborious method called 'dragging', which involved trying frequently used German words against every position in the cipher text. Peter and I used another method we created – the more instinctive approach, visibly different from Denis's dragging method. He was a senior teacher at Uppingham, the well-known public school. After the war he returned to Uppingham and continued to teach there.

Victor Masters, the third main shift leader, was aged about 35. We were on different shifts and I had little or no contact with him. A civilian with a business background, he returned to it after the war.

Peter Benenson had a rather minimal knowledge of German but he still managed to break a number of useful messages. Later in life, he became better known as the founder of the human rights group Amnesty (now Amnesty International), which he ran for a number of years before passing it on to others. This was an extremely valuable initiative – the activity of Amnesty, which helps political victims, has now spread worldwide and in the years since 1960, when it was formed, it must have helped millions of people. Yet it all goes back to Peter Benenson, a rather shy and modest lawyer. He died in 2005.

Peter Hilton, a mathematician and codebreaker, was the only person who liaised between the Testery and the Newmanry. His German was sketchy, but he used it well to break some of the standard messages, contributing solutions to the problems that arose when the Germans made changes in their use of Lorenz. Peter emigrated to the USA after the war and later became Distinguished Professor Emeritus of Mathematics at the State University of New York. He died in 2010, in the USA.

Roy Jenkins was another newcomer, in 1944. Roy was not good at codebreaking, because he had no German and no knack. He started as a wheelsetter, did well at that and was promoted to message breaker. After three months, however, he had little or no success. He recognised that he was not suited to the role and volunteered to go back to his earlier position as a wheelsetter. In later life, of course, he became Lord Jenkins of Hillhead, President of the Liberal Democrats, an outstanding politician, distinguished historian and a successful author. He was one of the few men who have held three top jobs in British government – Foreign Secretary, Home Secretary and Chancellor of the Exchequer. He died in 2003.

Donald Michie joined the Testery at a very young age – just 18. He came straight from school where his outstanding brilliance in mathematics had already been recognised. After a few months he was transferred to the Newmanry. He also contributed solutions to the problems that arose when the Germans made changes in their use of the Lorenz machine. Later he became a distinguished university professor. He died in 2007 in a car accident.

Bill Tutte was an excellent mathematician and codebreaker. He broke the twelve wheels of the Lorenz system in the spring of 1942, a method of working out the chi wheels from scratch on a two-message depth of 4,000 characters long, which then allowed the psi wheels and motor wheels to be worked out. Lorenz encrypted clear text three times. Tutte's break of the Lorenz system was an almost unbelievable achievement: he was a real genius.

Arthur Levenson (from the US Army) was an American visitor in the Testery and spent most of his time in Room 41 with us breakers. He was there to sit on our shoulders, study what we did and report on it to his superiors. Levenson was a man of considerable charm, so everybody got on well with him. He was allowed to study everything by special agreement between the British and the American authorities. The majority of operations during the war were conducted with allies, especially with America. Bletchley Park, however, was a complete exception to this. It was a strictly British operation.

One day, approximately ten years ago, I was amazed to see Arthur on the TV screen, appearing on the 1999 Channel 4 documentary *Station X*. He was talking about his work at Bletchley Park during the war. When this programme cropped up on Channel 4, he looked very much the same as he had done all those years before and I recognised him quite clearly. However, he never actually did any codebreaking.

2. Back-up Staff

After the codebreakers had broken their messages, the backroom staff followed on and carried out the other stages, such as working out the wheel patterns, identifying the start point on each wheel and deciphering the messages – very important, but often very boring and using very slow manual processes. There were a few groups made up mainly of non-commissioned army personnel who dealt with the more detailed work of registering traffic in and out, and other administrative tasks. When a break was established, it could occur at any point in the message, not necessarily at the beginning.

Room 41 was very close to the wheelsetters' Room 40 unit, so we could pass on details of a break for them to work on quickly. The wheelsetters' job was to work out the start points. Sometimes they might need to extend the break for a few more characters, so that they had enough material to pinpoint exactly the right place on each of the wheels – the five psi wheels, then the two motor wheels and the five chi wheels (at a later stage this was taken over by the Newmanry's machines). Thereafter, they traced back to the beginning of the message and established start points on each of the wheels; these were then given to the ATS team.

There were two people in particular who worked on all of this right from the start: 'Tubby' Roots and Jim Walford. They did a really sterling job in the Testery, including the 'Turingery'. The work was enormously laborious and unglamorous, but vital. I greatly respected the massive contribution these two made.

Later, the work was split up into separate elements and more staff were recruited for each of the three shifts. In the end, the back-up staff occupied eight separate spaces in the Testery, within Block F.

3. The ATS Team

Some twenty-four ATS women worked in Room 27. They dealt with the typing of the clean copies of the decrypted messages. Helen Pollard was the first person to be taken on and was promoted to staff sergeant. Another ATS girl, Ann Bridgewater, stood out for her quality as a person and her quiet capability and she was eventually given a well-deserved commission.

Once the ATS girls had received the start point, they would plug it up on a British Tunny machine (a machine created by the British to decode the cipher text from the Germans' Lorenz machine) and then type in the cipher text so that the clear text would be produced. They would have already plugged up the wheel pattern of the day on their machines.

None of us had had any experience of anything at all similar before the war. The best example of this is the ATS team, who had to adapt to typing on their Tunny machines, which operated in a completely different way to ordinary typewriters. In spite of this, there were never any grumbles or complaints at the difficulty of the work, even though none of the girls spoke German and were working completely in a language they could not understand.

4. The Management

Ralph Tester was head of the overall unit and a German linguist. He was a pipe smoker, aged 40ish. He made major decisions and represented the Testery vis-à-vis other departments at Bletchley Park or elsewhere. He was recruited to Bletchley at the same time as I was and he came from Unilever, where he had a senior position in their accountancy division.

The work of the unit was very well organised. The personnel were well selected and the unit seemed to find a right place for everybody. It was very rare to see members of the unit with nothing to do, absences were minimal and the work spirit was good. The atmosphere in the unit was always positive and friendly. The excellent organisation of the Testery was due in good part to the friendly but firm urbanity of the imperturbable Tester himself, who was greatly assisted in management by another senior man, Tom Colvill.

Tom Colvill was in his 30s and he was the unit's general manager. He had previously been a manager in a major insurance company. As Tester spent more time liaising with other departments, Tom handled progressively more of the management side. Any personnel problems, and most personal ones, were dealt with by Tom. There was enough to keep him busy, but there were very few problems that came to my knowledge. A lot of the credit for the successful handling of the very diverse talents and types of people in the team must go to Tom Colvill. He eventually bore the burden of the admin generated by 118 employees – a number you would expect in a quite sizeable commercial company.

After the war, both Tester and Colvill returned to their respective companies. Tester died in 1998, aged 95. Colvill died in the same year. Mei and I went to both their funeral services.

WHAT DID THE TESTERY DO DAILY?

In the earlier stages, the support staff in the Testery were responsible for preparing two messages with the same encryption; they would write them out one on top of the other and add them together to make a key and pass this on to cryptographers. When we added the two cipher texts together, we then had to break that key, producing the two original messages in the clear text. Clear text was the original unencoded message as it was meant to be read.

The key was the addition of two cipher texts that had been enciphered in the same way. When you got two messages with the same encryption, you would carefully write the first 500 letters of message one and, immediately underneath, 500 letters of message two and add them together to get the 'key'. The Germans must have realised this potential weakness in the system and that is why they made a major change. They insisted that every new message was encrypted using new wheel settings.

The cryptographer would then try 'Roem' (short for *Roemisch* in German, meaning Roman numbers). A lot of units in the German Army were assigned Roman numerals – I, II and so on. These could not be typed as they stood and the Lorenz operator handled them by typing the German equivalent of 'Roman 1'. The abbreviation therefore cropped up a lot. (This is covered in more detail in the section of Chapter 10 titled 'Breaking: Early Days')

Roem was used frequently in text or some other 'crib', moving along the letters and testing for the key to see whether it threw up other German clear text. If we found the right place, it would show a bit of good German from the second message. The codebreakers would then work on this backwards and forwards to keep extending the break until we had the number of places we needed. When you struck a 'roem' and added that to the key and you had selected the right place, a recognisable piece of German text would be produced instead of nonsense. The codebreakers had to keep testing all the time, rejecting the results until the right place gave a German word, or part of a word, then they knew they had a break.

This is how we were able to work until autumn 1943, when the supply started to drop off, until 1 January 1944 and then there were no more depths at all. Clearly the Germans had issued firm instructions to change the wheel start points for every message. There were hardly any exceptions from that point on and this generated a great deal of work for the Testery, so the staff in each department was increased substantially.

We had to use a quite different technique, a more complicated method which Tutte worked out for us. We had to change the wheel setting of every single message. This meant we could only break one message at a time – this was tougher, but we quickly adapted to the new situation. Meanwhile, the Testery had to apply a new method for breaking the individual messages. When a crib was added to a single message at the right place, the result was to produce the stuttering patterns of psi wheels. This was a lot more difficult for the codebreakers than working with depths, but after a short time we became used to looking for the stuttering patterns instead of text and the percentage of messages broken went back up again to the previous level.

The new technique used by the codebreakers was to look for groups of letters or repeated characters such as KKKHHPPPP333TT and so on. Once we saw this pattern, we knew we had a break. This was extended in the normal way until we had about fifty consecutive letters of text to work out the new wheel pattern. The codebreakers then had to do a second task on each of the messages to break around twenty to twenty-five consecutive places which allowed the wheelsetters to establish the start points for the messages on each of the wheels. At first, this was quite difficult for the codebreakers, but we soon got used to fishing for the new patterns instead of using German text. The proportion of messages broken went back to around 90 per cent. This remained the system until the end of the war.

In early 1944, the number of messages increased very sharply, especially on the Russian fronts. This increased volume meant that we had to have more hands to do the breaking of messages and all the other steps that followed, and, as a result, each part of the Testery was augmented considerably. A number of recruits were brought in – about six more codebreakers, mostly with some knowledge of the German language. Although talented, they did not have the depth of experience that we – the three original senior cryptographers – had enjoyed.

As we broke one message we looked forwards eagerly to the next one. It was a constant challenge. The progress of the new recruits was slow and some did not enjoy the work. In particular, they still had to learn the 992 combinations. But even when they did, they still had to acquire the skill and the 'knack' of finding the break-ins. Nonetheless, they added significantly to the total number of messages broken.

We did not need to break the whole message; we broke enough of it to work out the wheel pattern of the day or to find the start position on each of the wheels. Mostly we did not see the rest of the message, because it was important to get it on its way to the people who would perform the next stages. The final stage involved giving the messages to our ATS girls and they would type the cipher text into their machines. Thousands of Lorenz messages were decoded by the ATS girls. We codebreakers spent little or no time in reading these messages; our obligation was to break yet more messages. We could not afford the luxury of spending time looking through the broken messages.

What constantly claimed our attention was the mess of still unbroken traffic. We could, of course, have spent time reminding ourselves of the language used by the Germans, but we had familiarised ourselves with this in the early months of breaking when we had more time. We realised fully that our obligation was to keep breaking the messages and we were reminded all the time how important the traffic was from the signatures of the people who sent the messages.

There were just a handful of officers in the German Army High Command, and there were no Toms, Dicks and Harrys among the generals. Starting in 1944, I can clearly recall breaking a number of messages signed by Hitler himself – 'Adolf9Hitler9Fuehrer9'. I still remember the thrill when I broke my first message signed by him, but the novelty soon wore off and they were soon treated like the rest. We were, of course, constantly seeing messages signed by the various top generals and field marshals such as Chief of Staff von Jodl, Field Marshal Warlimont (deputy to von Jodl), von Weichs, Field Marshal Kesselring, Field Marshal Rommel, and so on. These were the main people in charge of the huge forces on the main battle fronts. For example, in Kursk, the German force numbered nearly 800,000 men. At least that gives an idea of what sort of messages we were breaking.

During the hand break period in early April 1943, Lorenz decrypts showed that the Germans were planning a huge assault at the city of Kursk, on the Eastern Front. We warned the Russians and then we told them how the attack was going to be made; specifically, that it would be a pincer attack. We also told them what units the Germans were going to use. The Germans planned to use a huge number of tanks, so the Russians laid hands on every single tank they could get and put pressure on their factories to produce and deliver yet more. This was the biggest tank battle in history, and the Russians managed to resist and push the Germans back. They called it the 'Turning of the Tide', when the Russians gained the upper hand on the Eastern Front for the remainder of the war. Lorenz decrypts played a very important part in this. If we had lost the Russians as allies, it would have been extremely serious and could have affected the war on the Western Front and D-Day very badly.

Another vital contribution made by breaking Lorenz occurred on the Western Front around D-Day. The critical question was where the bulk of the German troops would be, either up in the Calais region or in the Normandy area. The German generals wanted them to be in the Normandy area, because they guessed the Allies would be landing there on the beaches, but Hitler had fallen for a trick the British had played. Hitler insisted the troops should be allocated in the Calais region for five days. This was absolute intelligence gold dust. The information had not come from spies, but directly from Hitler via Lorenz decrypts, in the German's own words – in black and white.

From the parts of the messages we read, my recollection is quite clear that Lorenz traffic covered a wide range of subjects including troop movements, casualty reports, ammunition stocks, training of personnel and so on. Most of the time, the value of the messages lay in the steady build-up of information about situations and developments, as well as in certain individual messages.

We focused on our job, which was to break as many messages as possible and provide as much valuable intelligence as we could. There was a large amount of fascinating information. It would have been interesting to read these messages, but we couldn't read them all as we just didn't have time to do that. We were too busy breaking further messages. It was an exciting time.

Once the ATS girls had fully deciphered their messages in the Testery they were rushed to Hut 3, the team that dealt with army intelligence.

Some of them were sent on to Hut 4, which dealt with naval intelligence. The messages were then translated and dispatched to London, where they were duly forwarded on to the correct recipient in the War Office or elsewhere. Quite a number of the messages were placed on Winston Churchill's desk, because he loved to be better informed than everybody else and to be ahead of the game. I saw this desk for myself a few years ago, when I visited the underground Cabinet War Rooms near Whitehall, now a fascinating museum.

LORENZ TRAFFIC THROUGH THE TESTERY

Organisation of the Material

The whole process went so quickly in the Testery that it is not impossible that our generals occasionally saw the contents of the Lorenz messages sooner than the German generals managed to read their own copies.

Every day, traffic came in from each of the various German Army groups on both the Western and Eastern fronts. The traffic had to be recorded and classified and a check kept on its progress right through to its machine decoding and the dispatch of the clear text to the intelligence officers in Huts 3 and 4. These functions and other aspects of practical organisation were the charge of the support staff – 'Tubby' Roots, assisted by Jim Walford and a small team. They prepared and brought in materials for the codebreakers. Roots was later promoted from staff sergeant to regimental sergeant major, the top non-commissioned rank, and Jim Walford from lance corporal to staff sergeant. They both deserved medals for sticking so well at their boring work. As the volume of traffic increased, the support staff were substantially reinforced from mid 1943 onwards.

Message Breaking

Messages were distributed to message breakers in Room 41 according to the day's priorities. There were two jobs for the codebreakers to do; the first involved finding a break of sufficient length of cipher text to allow the wheel patterns to be established, usually by stretching backwards and forwards along the cipher text. It was necessary to break up to fifty consecutive places of the German cipher text. Even when you had a very good knowledge of the German language it was still quite challenging. This was to make a so-called 'key' by adding together two cipher texts that were thought to be in depth, that is, enciphered on the same wheel settings. The clear text of the two messages, when added together gave the same 'key'. The codebreakers' second task on each of the messages was to break around twenty to twenty-five consecutive places, which allowed the wheelsetters to establish the start points for the messages on each of the twelve wheels.

When a codebreaker obtained a break-in, it could occur at any point in the message, not necessarily at the beginning. They would then pass the break on to a wheelsetter in the team in Room 40, next door to the breakers. They had the task of working the clear text back to the beginning of the message so that the starting positions of the wheels could be established. Where the wheel patterns were already known, they had to identify at what point on each of the twelve wheels the message began. This is the task known as 'wheelsetting'. Once identified, the details were passed on to the ATS team.

Machine Decoding

The ATS team would plug up the start point on their British Tunny machines. The messages would be decrypted and this produced the final clear text in German. The messages were then passed on to the appropriate department, most often Hut 3 for German Army traffic. As an ATS girl typed in the cipher text, so the clear text came out on a tape. If all went well, the British Lorenz machine would reverse the process of encryption that had been carried out by the German Lorenz machine and the clear text would come bubbling out of the automatic typewriter. We could enter the cipher text and the original message would emerge – magic! It was an extraordinary thing to observe. Our Lorenz machines were doing exactly what the German machines could do.

In the early days, we did everything by hand. It wasn't until mid 1943 that we started to have British Tunny machines installed in the

Testery to do the final deciphering. By early 1944 as many as ten machines arrived, staffed by the team of ATS girls. The British Tunny machine did the mechanical deciphering of the messages – the final stage, but not the original basic codebreaking.

On each shift, a team of seven or eight ATS girls carried out the typing process, hammering away at their machines for eight or nine hours at a stretch. The night-watch, from midnight to 9 a.m., was particularly demanding. There was a break for forty minutes around 4 a.m., and on a snowy or rainy night the 100-yard or so walk or dash to the canteen rather took the shine off the break – the more so as the limited wartime food available reduced the appeal further. The canteen cooks did their best but there were severe limits to what could be done with the wartime rations.

When the war was in its final stages, at the end of 1944–45, the workload became very heavy due to the increased frequency of messages as the Germans retreated to their own territory. Then VE Day came in May 1945.

10

HOW HAND BREAKING WORKED

BREAKING LORENZ TRAFFIC – THE BASIC ELEMENTS

How the Baudot Alphabet Worked

The SZ40/42 cipher machine *Schlüsselzusatz* ('special attachment') produced cipher text by adding another letter to each letter in the message, then used a teleprinter code (also called the Baudot code) for transmitting the message via a teleprinter. The Baudot code represented every letter and a number of symbols by five electrical pulses (dot and cross [• and x]), allowing a total of thirty-two characters to be represented. It was this code that was used in all of the Lorenz messages.

Knowledge of this code was an absolute basic element for cryptographers in the breaking of Lorenz messages. As an example, the letter A was represented as: pulse, pulse, no pulse, no pulse, no pulse (or x x • • •), the letter B was x • • x x, the letter G was • x • x x, and so on. In modern-day computer terms, the 'pulse' and 'no pulse' can be thought of as data 'bits' and the state of each dot can take one of only two values (a binary system) that can be represented by 'True' and 'False' or '1' and '0'. But of course, this was the early days of computing and such terminology hadn't been invented then.

It was this wheel pattern which produced the chi and psi streams. When a key was pressed at the keyboard or a letter read from the tape in 'auto' mode, the five chi wheels turned in unison allowing one cam on each code wheel to pass its switch. The pattern of five electrical pulses and non-pulses, produced at this point by the code wheels created a letter in teleprinter code, for example x x • • • or the letter A. The five psi wheels also produced a letter which was added to that created by the chi wheels to produce a character of the key stream.

The Lorenz teleprinter system was based on the international Baudot code, which uses a series of five 'dots' to encode twenty-six letters of the alphabet and six special characters – thirty-two in all.

How the Letter Addition Worked

Two dot symbols or two cross symbols cancelled each other out to make a dot, while a dot plus a cross made a cross:

```
x + x = • (cross + cross = dot)
• + • = • (dot + dot = dot)
x + • = x (cross + dot = cross)
• + x = x (dot + cross = cross)
```

Further characters and symbols could be represented by the teleprinter code (e.g. numbers) by preceding the sequence with 'control' codes that effectively instructed the teleprinter to switch to a different symbol set.

At the end of the stream of alternative characters, another control code would switch the teleprinter back to the normal symbol set. For instance, a full stop was shown as 55M889, where 55 would mean 'I am going into punctuation', M meant 'full stop', 88 meant 'I am coming out of it and back to the ordinary text' and 9 always indicated a space. If a comma was to be used instead, then the M would be replaced by N. M was used very frequently in German text; it was the crib most frequently used by the codebreakers to get the first break-in.

Numbers were often shown in the same way. Thus, 1 was shown as 55Q889; 2 used W instead of Q; 4 would be shown as 55R889, and so on.

How Lorenz Encrypted

In the Baudot code system, it was possible to add two characters together to create another letter (or other symbol character, such as A + B = G). For example, adding A and B gives • x • x x, which is the representation for the character G, as shown below:

Character addition representation:	Addition of the bit pattern representation of the characters:
A	X X • • •
B	X • • X X
G	• X • X X

How Lorenz Decrypted

In the decipherment process, a letter (or other symbol character) of the clear text would have a cipher letter added to it by the Lorenz machine which produced the cipher text letter. If the same cipher letter was added to the cipher text letter then the result would be the original clear text letter. For example, adding B to A produces G, then adding G to B takes it back to A:

Character addition representation:	Addition of the bit pattern representation of the characters:
G	• X • X X
B	X • • X X
A	X X • • •

This leads to a large number of 'triplets' like this. We codebreakers had to know them by heart.

However, it is worth mentioning that a teleprinter tape used the Baudot code and looked like this (with the arrangement of holes and spaces representing each character aligned across the width of the tape. There was also a row of sprocket holes running the entire length of the tape between rows 2 and 3 of the characters, that are not depicted in the following simplified representation):

```
o o . o o o . . . o
o . o . . . o . o o
. . o . . o . o o o
. o o o . o o . . o
. o . . . . o o . .
A B C D E F G H I J … etc.
```

The os are holes punched in the tape. We always represented the holes, when writing them down, with an 'x', it was easier. This system used twenty-six different letters plus six other symbols and numbers, exactly the same system as is used on a typewriter today – 1234567890 and underneath, the letters QWERTYUIOP.

Since it is part of the Baudot code system which was used in the Testery, the German enciphering of messages was decrypted at every stage by hand in the Testery. But later on we were able to add electronically to the plain text using chi wheels, one to cover each of the five wheels, to speed up one stage of the process of the breaking. (The combining of the cross and dots of two letters in this encoding / decoding method is called 'modulo-2 addition' and can be achieved using the bit-wise logic function of 'Exclusive-Or' or 'XOR' in modern computing terminology.)

How the 992 Combination Worked

Another basic and important element for the cryptographers was to be able to instantly recall each of the 992 combinations in the breaking of Lorenz. These were all the possible combinations of each character of the Baudot code added to all other characters of the code. There were 992 possible pairs you could make out of thirty-two characters. There were twenty-six alphabet letters, plus six other characters (3, 4, /, 5, 8, 9) – altogether thirty-two. Each of these characters (32) could combine with each of the others (31), but you could not combine any one character with itself, which meant the number of different pairs of characters is mathematically 32 x 31 = 992.

Since there were thirty-two characters only, they were represented in Baudot code. Each pair of characters can be added to another to give a third, as described above, adding A to B would give G, adding G to B would give A, and adding B to A would give G. We had to be able to look at any two of the thirty-two characters and know immediately what the character would add up to, because A, B and G are permanently linked with 992 combinations. From this basic knowledge, we codebreakers would fit the message onto the wheel patterns of that day to break them. We would then try to extend it forwards and back, normally up to fifty characters, until we had enough to find each of the twelve wheel positions. Then we would pass on the break to the wheelsetters to decipher the whole message.

The letter to be enciphered was first overlaid by the five chi wheels and then overlaid by the psi wheels, but the five psi wheels were controlled by the two motor wheels and they were always changing. In effect, you had three changes applied whenever you produced a letter. This is how the clear text of the message was three times encrypted. Each time the change could be any one of the thirty-two characters, and as we know, these could be paired in 992 different combinations. The cryptographers had to know all of these instantly by heart or by eye.

Peter Ericsson and I were the champions at breaking messages because we knew the 992 combinations so well and our reactions were faster than others. We also had a good knowledge of German, which was essential. But as well we both seemed to have the knack of spotting break-ins. The linguists came to know more and more of the military language used in these messages and built knowledge about potential cribs, so it was a case of success leading to further success. We always worked hard with great energy and enthusiasm, because we enjoyed the game so much. There was indeed a great sense of excitement as each of the break-ins began and was extended successfully.

Peter and I would look for frequently used beginnings and endings to often used German expressions. We were constantly on the alert for bits like '9ge-' or '-ung9', '-te9', and so on, along with dozens of others. We were thus hunting for many possible break-ins at the same time. We also seemed to have a cryptographer's instinct for break-ins. This kind of instinct is difficult to explain but one can just feel it.

Denis Oswald, the third senior codebreaker, was a good all-rounder, but he used the more laborious method of 'dragging'. He was a methodical person, and the others all used the same method as Denis, except Peter and I. Later on, by the middle of 1943, as the workload became heavier, the twenty or so slower members of the team all together made a useful total contribution to the number of messages broken. The breaking of messages was an experience and such an adventure, especially the more difficult ones which were more challenging for us. And so, every day we had to keep trying, trying, testing, testing, all the time, until we got the break-in.

This kind of daily work of hand breaking in the Testery was in our blood and every day the work was extremely demanding and challenging, but very satisfying. I could not get away from these combinations and break-ins, even when I was on leave. More than seventy years later, I still can recall all the combinations instantly. Sometimes when I am sitting in the car, I still find myself trying to 'break' car number plates with 9ROEM9 or 55M889 (the code for a full stop). I often tell my wife, 'that car number plate has got an almost perfect "Roem"'.

Roy Jenkins had no knowledge of German and no knack; this made it frustrating for him when he tried to tackle a message. He was drafted into the Testery probably because of his background rather than any potential cryptographic talent. His father had been a well-known Labour MP. There was never any doubt as to what Roy would become in later life. However, Roy greatly admired the breakers; he described them well in his autobiography, *A Life at the Centre* (Macmillan, 1991): 'Tester's section was divided into two parts. There were the "breakers" and the "setters". The breakers were obviously the elite. They were like matadors compared with picadors.'

He also gave his recollection of his own feelings:

I went to a dismal breakfast having played with a dozen or more messages and completely failed with all of them. It was the most frustrating mental experience I have ever had, particularly as that act of trying almost physically hurt one's brain, which became distinctly raw if it was not relieved by the catharsis of achievement.

I used to meet Roy occasionally after the war. In the late 1990s Roy and I started contacting each other again, and he gave me a signed a copy of his autobiography. He invited me a number of times to have a drink at the House of Lords and also visited me at my London home in Belgravia. That contact with him all happened before the declassification of Lorenz so we did not talk about it at all.

Roy and I got on very well together – we were born within a week of each other. However, there was a gap in our correspondence and in a later letter he explained he had been in hospital recovering from a serious heart operation. Sadly, he died a year later in 2003. I do wish, from all points of view, that he had lived longer. He would have been a valuable ally for me in my campaign to get better recognition for the three Ts – Tutte, Tunny and the Testery. He had many of the right contacts, political and otherwise, and of course he was a wonderful and very talented person to know.

How Lorenz's Twelve Wheels Functioned

The set of five chi wheels changed the clear text letters to a new letter for each new letter to be encoded. This new letter in turn was changed a second time by the set of five psi wheels, but the psi wheels were subject to the control of the two motor wheels. These motor wheels sometimes stopped the psi wheels on and sometimes had no effect. However, the next time the psi wheels came around it wouldn't be the same, because the motor wheels had their own patterns.

The clear text affected by the three sets of wheels had now become the cipher text. That meant the original clear text letter had been subjected to the three levels of encryption. We can really appreciate just how remarkable Tutte's achievement was. Such a three-level encryption must be very rare in cryptography – possibly even unique.

When breaking the messages, you had to bear in mind that you could not say, 'I am going to do exactly the same as before', since it would not work. In the early days, the Germans did not change the wheel patterns (which in modern terminology would be referred to as the key) on a daily basis, but as the war progressed, from 1943 onwards they changed the wheel patterns more frequently. From

1 January 1944 onwards, they were changed every day. So we found ourselves having to break new sets of wheel patterns daily – this was extremely challenging.

For example, the word 'eye' would be reproduced as below:

E Y E

X X X

• • •

• X •

• • •

• X •

Thus 'eye' would be affected in the following way given the chi wheels' positions we've taken as an illustration:

Text	With Chi wheels	Becomes cipher text
X X X	• X X	X • •
• • •	X • X	X • X
• X •	• X X	• • X
• • •	X • •	X • •
• X •	• • •	• X •
E Y E	R S U	J T I

This, in turn, was changed by the psi wheels. Let us assume that the psi wheels produce the three letters C Z Z (the second and third letters are both Z because the motor wheels have caused the psi wheels to stop for one character position). Notice that the two Es in the clear text have become S and Q in the cipher text:

• X X	Becomes	X X X	
X • •	(The third place is	• • X	So the two Es
X • •	also Z because the	X • X	in the clear text
X • •	motor wheels have	• • •	have become
• X X	caused the Psi wheels	• • X	S and Q in the
C Z Z	to stop one place)	S E Q	cipher text.

A chi or psi wheel might, for instance, look like this for its first eleven places: • • X X • • • X X • • and so on.

The full set of twelve wheels' lengths (i.e. the number of positions on each of the wheels) were:

Wheel number	Chi Wheels	Motor Wheels	Psi Wheels
1	41	61	43
2	31	37	47
3	29		51
4	26		53
5	23		59

Thus all but chi wheel 4 and psi wheel 3 were prime numbers.

BREAKING THE CHI WHEELS: FIRST, ALL BY HAND THEN ASSISTED BY MACHINE

During the first year of breaking Lorenz, the Testery cryptographers and support staff broke every message and every stage by hand, using depths which had been reasonably plentiful. We used the Turingery method to establish the patterns of the chi wheels (it was Turing who devised the first systematic method for reading the traffic). It was the only effective method of breaking the chi wheels during that period. Breaking each Lorenz message involved seven stages of work, and each message might take anything from three hours up to a whole day in the first six months, depending on the skill of the codebreaker. The actual breaking of the German text was not all that difficult; it was the subsequent processes which often took the time, in particular the breaking of the chi wheels.

Fortunately, somebody realised that this process could be automated more quickly than could be done by hand. This was made possible by Dr Max Newman, who came to work in the Testery for three months. He did not know much of the German language; it was hard for him and he disliked the Testery's hand methods. He broke away from the Testery, set up his own department called the Newmanry in mid 1943, and proposed an approach using a machine.

After six months, the first of these machines became available to speed up the breaking of the chi wheels. It was called the ('Heath') Robinson (after the cartoonist, who sketched crazy machines), but it was slow and unreliable. We continued to break the chi wheels by hand for another six months or so, until a new machine was produced called Colossus, so called because of the huge size of the machine – it almost occupied a whole room. The first model of Colossus in early 1944 wasn't that sophisticated, but a later model came into service which helped to identify the chi wheel patterns faster and more reliably. We broke messages by hand in the Testery for nineteen months before Colossus came on stream.

The Newmanry's team, in developing machines for tacking single messages, brought about a major change in the work of the Testery. The work on Robinson had additional value, because it enabled the Testery to improve its techniques for breaking single messages before the sharp increase in the volume of messages from January 1944 onwards.

Colossus Mk 1 arrived at Bletchley Park in December 1943 and was fully operational by February 1944. It worked twice as fast as the Robinson. Then Colossus Mk 2 came into action in June 1944, just before D-Day. It was much faster: about five times faster than the Mk 1 model and ten times faster than the Robinson. By now, thousands of chi wheel settings were being broken in Room 41 by the codebreakers. With the Newmanry's help, the Testery success rate in message breaking reached over 90 per cent. It was a very busy period from then on.

I always thought the balance of credit given to the codebreakers in the Testery compared to that given to the machines in the Newmanry in breaking Lorenz was unfairly skewed towards the Newmanry. The Testery had been breaking large quantities of Lorenz messages by hand long before Colossus was produced. Even then, Colossus Mk 1 would have been useless without the manual codebreakers in the Testery. The Newmanry needed to know the chi wheel patterns before Colossus could be used to strip off the first layer of encryption. The chi wheel patterns were supplied to Colossus by the manual efforts of the codebreakers in the Testery. It wasn't until after D-Day in June 1944 that Colossus started to help the codebreakers out with the chi wheels.

BREAKING: EARLY DAYS

In the early days, the Germans made infrequent changes to their wheel settings. They would send a number of messages using the same wheel settings. This, of course, is a cardinal sin in cryptography. The result is called a 'depth' and can allow the enemy (in this case, us) to study repeated patterns. A depth is when two messages have the same encryption settings but differ slightly in content. This is how Colonel Tiltman got the 4,000 characters of cipher text. He wasn't able to break the two messages in depth or to read them, so the job was passed to Bill Tutte, who managed to reason it all out.

The German operators were supposed to change the wheel settings for every message they sent out, but they often ignored them for days. This created many depths; they were not supposed to do that, as depths are easier for codebreakers to break than single messages. During the early use of Lorenz, the Germans failed to change the wheel settings every day because they had so much confidence in their machines and did not expect anyone to be able to break them.

In the Testery, the two cipher texts (depths) were added to make a key. The codebreakers then looked for clear text in one that could give clear text in the other. When we found the right position, we knew we had a start. We then had to use our knowledge of German until we had enough consecutive places. It was necessary to build up at least fifty or so consecutive places of continuous clear text in each message for a full break to be established. This allowed the codebreakers to work out the settings and patterns of all twelve wheels. In the earlier days, from 1942 to the end of 1943, there were plenty of 'depths'.

Below is an example of a break showing how the process worked. The addition of the two cipher texts might produce, for example, … F J M 5 X E K L R J J … (… to extend the clear text, forwards and backwards). The cryptographer would test certain words against this and, if lucky, would find at one position that it gave possible clear text in the other message of the pair. For instance, F J M 5 X E K (the result of adding the two cipher texts). If I tried '9ROEM9' (Roman), I got out DE and GES, possible fragments of German:

```
9 R O E M 9
D E 9 G E S
```

German practices in particular were a godsend to the Testery due to the treatment of Roman numerals as discussed above. If one identified a likely sequence for 9ROEM9, one then had a run of six or more places we could follow up with a number – for instance, EINS (German for the number one), giving us four more places. The German operators used 9 to indicate a space between words, e.g. 9ROEM9EINS9. This looked like possible clear text. ROEM EINS meant 'Roman 1' and this find often indicated good German clear text:

```
F J M 5 X E K L R J J
9 R O E M 9 E I N S 9
D E 9 G E S C H I C K
```

The cryptographer would make an assumption that the message might include '9WURDE9GESCHICKT9' (i.e. *wurde geschickt*, which means 'was sent', in German) and see what letters that gave in the first message. If *wurde* ('was') did not work, he would try other likely words.

This obviously looked like possible clear text and so the cryptographer would push on with a number after ROEM and could perhaps have seen more clear text as below:

Cipher one	E S 8 G S C S 9 N P 5
Cipher two	N C A E 9 K R P I X T
Cipher one + two	F J M 5 X E K L R J J (the key)
Clear text one	9 R O E M 9 E I N S 9
Clear text two	D E 9 G E S C H I C K (… extend)

We would try to extend the break-in forwards and backwards (represented in the table by '…'), and keep testing and trying the break both ways until we got the length we needed.

We cryptographers had to have all the letter 'additions' (such as, A + B = G, F + 9 = D and so on) memorised and would have instantly at our fingertips all the 992 combinations. As soon as we saw a good clear text, we knew we had a break-in. The whole vocabulary of military German became second nature to us cryptanalysts. My German was good enough to deal with extending a break, but there were some messages where it was difficult to effect a break-in, so I would try to make a number of small break-ins and then seek to join them up. I could then very quickly test out possible clear texts, discard them if gibberish and try new ones. It was a thrilling feeling when you got a break-in, especially when you knew it could be an important message, based on the signature.

It was here, of course, where the linguists were most needed. A break-in might produce, for example, HEITEN9 (a frequent ending in German) and the linguists would try various likely words in order to extend the break, such as EINHEITEN (units). There were other frequent endings and the linguist would have to test out the various possibilities. Examples included:

UNGEN9 might be part of 9SENDUNGEN9 ('*sendungen*' = messages)
KEIT9 might be part of 9TAETIGKEIT9 ('*taetigkeit*' or *tätigkeit*' = activity).

If they did not prove correct, the codebreaker would think of other words and try again. The breaker had to look for a whole variety of such pieces of text and rapidly test them at different places in the cipher text. In the end, we might develop a kind of instinct for spotting a break-in or recognise a cluster of cipher letters which were the addition of two standard bits of clear text:

8 Z 9 V A /   (cipher letters)
9 R O E M 9   (Roman)
5 5 M 8 8 9   (full stop)

It looks easy but is not; you need good skills, good German, a good memory and the 'knack'. Some messages did prove relatively easy, especially if they had a lot of punctuation in them. Most messages were broken in anything from half an hour up to eight hours (a shift), but there were others which resisted for quite a long time – though rarely for more than twenty-four hours. These occasional 'toughies' could cause frustration and even desolation. Most of the time I could manage these, but for the others it would be hard going and we senior codebreakers quite often had to help them. Once enough text had been broken, it was necessary to work out the patterns for each of the twelve wheels in detail.

Example of Breaking Two Lorenz Messages in Depth

When we received a depth, the two cipher texts were added up to make a stream of letters. Then we tested typical German words at different points of the joined stream. If we found the right place, we would see good German (clear text) in the second message; if not, we would see gibberish. Most of the time we saw gibberish, so we would have to keep testing until we saw clear text, sometimes taking many hours.

Here is an example of how such a break-in might proceed:

The two cipher texts are added together to obtain clear text messages one and two:

```
J T S N Z 4 V E 4 C H C V F O D J S P 9 /
                  9 R O E M 9                    (clear text one)
                  T 9 I N 9 F                    (clear text two)
```

The First Extension: ROEM was always followed by a number, in this case 'EINS' (German for 'one'):

```
J T S N Z 4 V E 4 C H C V F O D J S P 9 /
                  9 R O E M 9 E I N S 9
                  T 9 I N 9 F R A G E 9
```

The Second Extension: The expression *in Frage* was often preceded by *kommt nicht* (*kommt nicht in Frage* – no question of retreat):

```
J T S N Z 4 V E 4 C H C V F O D J S P 9 /
              I L U N G 9 R O E M 9 E I N S 9
              9 N I C H T 9 I N 9 F R A G E 9
```

The Third Extension: ILUNG is the end of a military word often used in these messages (*Abteilung* – unit):

```
J T S N Z 4 V E 4 C H C V F O D J S P 9 /
9 A B T E I L U N G 9 R O E M 9 E I N S 9
K O M M T 9 N I C H T 9 I N 9 F R A G E 9
```

Towards the end of 1943, the Germans tightened up their procedures and there were no more depths. All messages were sent on different settings and so were enciphered differently. A new way of breaking had to be invented and luckily it was, by Bill Tutte. The Testery then carried on with the new method, but it is too complex to explain easily in this book. It is very difficult to explain how to break messages. Even when you have good knowledge of the German language and the skill, you still needed a kind of 'knack'. The trick was to follow that instinct.

To avoid an enemy picking up the text, the Germans normally used a number of *quatsch* ('rubbish') words or phrases at the beginning of the transmission, such as *heute moerderische Hitze* ('terribly hot today'). Some messages added this as an instruction for the operator at the other end, but we soon learned to recognise that this kind of expression was not a part of the real message.

Where the Germans had modified their procedures for the Lorenz machine, the Testery or the Newmanry had to establish what change the Germans had made and how we needed to change our approach to counteract it, so as to read their traffic again. The Germans made three main changes, which greatly affected our work:

Changing wheel patterns: Initially, they changed their wheel patterns infrequently, but from 1 January 1944 there were no more 'depths'. So us hand breakers now had a lot more work to do each day to break the wheel settings used on the new system. However, once Tutte found a solution to this, we could carry on with the new method, breaking daily again.

Changing the start point, which affected every message: Now we had to break every twenty or so places on every single message to establish the start points. As a result, the Testery had to recruit more message breakers and each of the follow-on stages also needed more staff. The Testery quickly grew in size, requiring more office space. The Newmanry also grew to add more machines to produce the de-chi stage.

A minor change on the fifth psi wheel: This stopped us at one point from breaking traffic at all until, luckily, the Germans found it led to so much trouble with their operators that they returned to the status quo. This blackout only lasted about two weeks. It caused temporary panic, but there was great relief when the Germans abandoned the change.

As the Germans opened more and more Lorenz links, the volume of traffic increased and the quantity of broken messages rose sharply. Up to mid 1943, for instance, a total of 1.5 million characters were decrypted (by hand methods) and the majority of depths were broken. On the 'singles' – i.e. messages not in depth – it was mostly not possible to effect a break, except when we had a 'crib'. Cribs included cases where we might guess that the message was a resend (using different wheel settings) of a message that we had already broken.

At the end of 1943, the Germans stopped sending the 'indicators' in clear text – i.e. not enciphered. Fortunately, Tutte, after a great deal of patient analysis, had managed to create a system for breaking the chi wheels on a single message, using a statistical approach.

BREAKING: LATER DAYS

From 1 January 1944, when the German operators tightened up their security procedures and the Testery no longer had any depths to rely on, the wheel patterns were changed every day. Our workloads increased significantly due to the increasing number of messages.

There was no longer a second message that we could use as a check against our efforts to produce plausible text. Instead, we had to use a different method for breaking into the messages from this time forwards. Now when we tested a piece of text, we would add it to the cipher text as before but this time it would produce a pattern similar to this:

HHHKKNNNN333RRR//SS ... etc.

If one identified a likely sequence for this expression, one then had a run of six or more places. If this clear text was added to the cipher text and this gave, for instance, a pattern of repeated letters like the following, you knew you had probably struck gold – i.e. the psi wheel's positions:

```
X  X  •  •  •  •  •  •
X  X  •  •  •  X  X  X
•  •  X  X  X  •  •  •
•  •  X  X  X  •  •  •
•  •  •  •  •  X  X  X
A  A  N  N  N  L  L  L
```

This emerging pattern was typical of the contribution of the psi wheels as 'stretched out' with repeated letters due to the action of the motor wheels.

A second highly useful practice was the way the Germans handled punctuation. The letter M was used as a full stop but, so that it would not be taken as part of a word, it was necessary to indicate its use as punctuation and this was done by using 55 going in and 88 coming out of punctuation mode. We always wrote ++ instead of 55, so at the end of a sentence, one might have + + M 8 8, or, with luck, 9 + + M 8 8 9, thereby giving, in the second example, seven places.

Other punctuation used a similar principle: a comma used N instead of M, a colon used C, and so on. Numbers were also rendered this way: QWERTYUIOP (the letters along the top row of the keyboard) were used respectively for 1, 2, 3, 4, 5, etc., thus + + W889 represented 2.

We would also look for bits of words in German which cropped up very often. Even a small group of three places could initiate a break-in. For example:

9VER – a lot of German verbs begin with these letters
TE9 – again, a lot of past tenses ended with this group of letters.

There were a number of commonly occurring word endings in German text and we might look for one of these:

-HEITE – such as '*einheit*' (unit)
-UNG – such as '*meldung*' (report)
EN-, KEIT, and a number of others.

It was not possible to test each of these in all locations, but a good cryptographer would have all these in his mind when he looked at the cipher text and have a kind of instinct which is very difficult to describe, to feel that a certain text belonged at a certain point. Quite often we would be correct. This was obviously a much quicker way of trying to establish a break-in. It meant juggling these very common groupings of letters in your mind as you looked at the cipher text – quite difficult to do, but extremely effective.

The emerging pattern looked like the five psi wheels when extended by the motor wheels. This seemed a great deal more difficult at first, but in the end it was similar in difficulty to the earlier method and we got used to it quite quickly. What we were doing was reproducing the actual psi pattern used in the message. If we broke something like fifty or more consecutive places of this, that would give us ten or more places of actual psi wheel patterns. Then we could look for the patterns on the psi wheels which we had already worked out.

After we broke the places for wheel patterns and the places for the start points, the wheelsetters could set to work establishing the start points for each of the psi wheels and motor wheels, work the message back to the beginning of it and establish the actual start points on each of the twelve wheels. This soon fell into a regular pattern of handling, which continued until the end of the war. However, the Testery was still responsible for carrying out the rest of the process by hand. We still worked out the patterns of the psi wheels and motor wheels and still had to carry out the final decryption of the messages.

It was now recognised by the senior staff at Bletchley Park that the breaking of Lorenz traffic was vital for the Allies. The Testery needed machines to help speed up one stage of the breaking process – the focus was on the breaking of the chi wheels. It was thought this stage could best be carried out by a machine since this stage was laborious, long and time consuming.

In mid 1943, Dr Max Newman was charged with tackling this problem. Luckily Colossus, the first large-scale electronic computer, came on stream at exactly this time. It was used to 'take off' the effect of the five chi wheels from the cipher text of a message. The resultant simplified cipher text, known as a 'de-chi' was then broken by the Testery to establish the settings of the other seven wheels (the five psi wheels and the two motor wheels which drove them). The Testery could then decipher these de-chi messages.

At first the Newmanry had only one Colossus, with a number of Wrens to operate the machines and a couple of engineers. Later the number rose, and ten were being used at Bletchley Park by the end of the war. From early 1944 until the war's end, the use of the machine was now essential.

Bear in mind that the use of Colossus was not for breaking Lorenz messages; it was used purely for breaking the chi wheel patterns and then removing their effect from the cipher text to make a de-chi. In other words, Colossus stripped away from the cipher text the contribution made by the chi wheel. In order to break the de-chis produced by hand, it was still necessary to establish the patterns of the psi wheels and the two motor wheels. We codebreakers in the Testery tried possible pieces of German text against it, attempting to generate what looked like a pattern of psi wheels.

THE SEVEN STAGES IN THE DAILY BREAKING OF LORENZ

From July 1942 to mid 1943, everything was processed by hand in the Testery using the seven stages outlined below.

The support staff in the Testery selected a pair of messages likely to have been enciphered using the same encryption – a 'depth' – with a good length and free from corruption. The two messages were added together to make a key.

The codebreaker then broke this key up to fifty places of cipher text for that day's patterns of the five chi wheels to be established.

The effect of the chi wheels was then removed from the cipher text to make so-called 'de-chi' messages, around twenty to twenty-five cipher texts for each individual message.

The message was then passed to the cryptographers/linguists. The cryptographers had to break around fifty consecutive places of the key to bring out the clear text of both messages.

In order to find out the start points on each of the twelve wheels, the codebreakers broke twenty to twenty-five consecutive places on each individual message.

Support staff subtracted the new 'clear text 1' from 'cipher text 1' to produce the psi stream. From this they then worked out the patterns of the five psi wheels and two motor wheels. The start point would come out automatically at the same time, to pinpoint exactly the right place on each of the twelve wheels.

These were then given to the ATS team. They plugged the patterns up on their Lorenz machines, typed in the cipher text and the German clear text was produced to reveal the original German message.

THE THREE PHASES IN THE DAILY BREAKING OF LORENZ

Phase 1, the Hand Breaking Period (mid 1942 to mid 1943)

Hand breaking Lorenz was a slow process, but very productive from an intelligence perspective. Since the Testery had been established, the quantity of German messages successfully broken amounted to approximately 1.5 million characters of cipher text. The Testery would also work out all three sets of twelve wheel patterns (chi wheels, psi wheels and motor wheels), allowing most of the day's targeted traffic to be deciphered. For a whole year, the Testery had to work out the wheel patterns, wheel settings and perform the deciphering completely by hand.

During this period, crucial messages were broken relating to the build-up of German troops at Kursk on the Russian Front. The Battle of Kursk is regarded as the 'turning of the tide' by the Russians, and from that point on it was also extremely important to Europe.

Phase 2, with Limited Help from the Robinson Machines (from mid 1943 to the end of 1943)

By mid 1943, the volume of decrypts had risen sharply as the use of Lorenz quickly spread to different links and fronts. Each of the different links, given a different fish code name by the Testery, used a different set of wheel patterns.

Four important things happened during this period:

1. From the middle of 1943, British Tunny machines were installed in the Testery and ATS girls were taken on to operate them. This greatly increased the speed of the deciphering process, which had previously been carried out manually.

2. A machine named ('Heath') Robinson was built, a precursor to Colossus. The Robinson machine was designed to play a key part in producing the de-chi, but the psi wheels and motor wheels would still have to be broken by hand in the Testery. The Robinson machine was slow and not too reliable and, in fact, right up to the end of 1943 the majority of Lorenz messages continued to be broken entirely by hand in the Testery.

3. The mathematical method used in the Robinson was invented by the great cryptanalyst Bill Tutte. Tutte's method was central to the operation of Robinson and, later, Colossus. Once the Robinson was operational, the new team became active from July 1943, under Dr Max Newman. The 'Newmanry' was staffed mainly by mathematicians who used machines to support the Testery, speeding up one stage of decryption – the breaking of the five chi wheels.

4. The Germans tightened up their procedures and the supply of depths steadily began to dry up. By the end of 1943, there were no more depths at all. Fortunately, Tutte's new method did not require depths. Thanks to Tutte, the Testery was able to continue breaking Lorenz until the end of the war.

Phase 3, with Help from Colossus
(15 February 1944 to the War's End)

In February 1944, a new machine became available: Colossus Mk 1, now recognised as the world's first programmable electronic computer. Designed and built in only ten months by Tommy Flowers, an engineer of the GPO (General Post Office), Colossus had a much greater capacity than Robinson, was more reliable and, because it was electronic, worked at a much higher speed, so the whole breaking process became faster.

Colossus Mk 2 came along at just the right time, before D-Day, because the Germans began to change the Lorenz wheel patterns ever more frequently and the volume of messages vastly increased. Hand methods could not have kept pace. Colossus had far greater capacity and speed compared to the Robinson. Colossus Mk 2 was essential for making the very fast counts needed to work out the de-chis. The Colossus machines were now essential in producing de-chis until the war's end. However, the psi wheels, motor wheels and the final deciphering still had to be carried out manually in the Testery.

The Testery was hand breaking Lorenz for twelve months before the Robinson machine was produced and for nineteen months before Colossus operated. Once again, the case shows that however important the machines later became, it needed the human mind to break the ground first. The regular breaking of Lorenz was a triumph of minds, not machines.

AN ORIGINAL LORENZ DECRYPT MESSAGE
FROM 1942

In 2013, Katherine Lynch, the media manager at Bletchley Park showed me a copy of an original Lorenz message (see plates). I was amazed to see it, since it is a rare artefact. It was quite exciting and it brought back old memories. I knew that all the paperwork on Lorenz had been destroyed at the end of the war on Churchill's orders, and yet this was a real Lorenz message broken and deciphered by the Testery in our unit.

It showed the final stage of the seven stages of the breaking process, after the codebreakers and the support staff had done their work. This clear text, of course, was in German. At this stage of the process I could have read the whole message if I had wanted to, but I did not have the time for such luxuries as I would have had to move on to breaking more messages.

This document was ready to send on to Hut 3 for translation and for dispatch to the right department. Here is my translation for you, showing the contents:

> IBIS reports on 12/8/42. According to a report dated 11/8, No. 1 Indian tank brigade is mutinying brigades on African Front; No. 10 emergency Indian Brigade and six Indian Inf. Brigade. 42 soldiers were shot; many officers and men were taken prisoner. All radio equipment was confiscated. Some of the troops withdrawn from front line. On 11/8, EL AMIRIYA landing grounds (25km south-west of Alexandria) there are 18 aircraft, mostly fighter-aircraft. The rest are reconnaissance and transport planes of English and American origins. Eight anti-aircraft guns secured, 5MG Berries, 10 Searchlights, four radio stations, available bombs and replacement magazines for aircraft. Source Rumania, No. 1 Air Commander. South has AST in the Military Zone Rumania. XVII BBNR 5267/42 secret. Rumania. I. H. FERNO. Leader Ast.

This kind of message cropped up every day, but was usually of a much higher level, especially when we had broken a message sent or received by one of the top German generals, field marshals or even one from Hitler. You can imagine how exciting it was.

TWO WEEKS' BLACKOUT IN 1944

During the second half of 1944, there was a two-week period when we could not read a single message, because the Germans had made changes to the way the Lorenz machine worked. The Germans allowed the five psi wheels to influence the enciphering process and this made it impossible for us to break Lorenz. We had nothing to work on and we were extremely worried. Fortunately for us, after the two-week black-out the extra procedure proved too troublesome for the Germans, which slowed down their operation. As a result, they decided to give it up and go back to the normal process, so the breaking of Lorenz continued as before. We were greatly relieved and so was Hut 3.

I can remember breaking messages about Kursk. We were able to warn the Russians that the attack was going to be launched and the fact that it was going to be a pincer movement. We had to wrap it all up and say it was from spies, to show that we had wonderful teams of spies. The decrypts from Lorenz were not from any old Tom, Dick or Harry but from the senior German generals and contained valuable information about the wider progress of the war.

Today, we codebreakers would have been regarded as superstars. In the last two years, I have given so many interviews, talks, articles, even TV programmes, including BBC News, about the breaking of Lorenz and my wartime experiences. But in those more egalitarian days, we were all on the same level as everyone else – people all doing their part of an important job. There was a great feeling of camaraderie in the Testery, engendered by the feeling that we were all working on something very important. In the circumstance of wartime, we all worked extremely hard, whether we fulfilled the role of codebreaker or support staff – everyone made their contribution, large or small, in breaking Lorenz as a team. The team achieved so much in the Testery.

11

HOW THE TESTERY WAS ASSISTED BY MACHINES

The Testery from autumn 1941 onwards was primarily made up of linguists, codebreakers, support staff and the ATS girls, under Ralph Tester. We were the only team tasked with the daily breaking of Lorenz.

The Newmanry, from July 1943 onwards, was primarily staffed by mathematicians, support staff and the Wren girls who later operated the Colossus machines, under Dr Max Newman. The Newmanry machines allowed us to break single messages instead of always needing two messages in depth. With the machine's help, we now broke the traffic faster, which led to major changes in the work of the Testery, speeding up one stage of the breaking process.

At first the Robinson machine, for six months from the middle of 1943, was slow and unreliable, so we still carried on doing everything by hand in the Testery. From early 1944, with Colossus the process became much faster. Colossus was essential for performing the high-speed counting on the chi wheels, thus speeding up the whole breaking process. Many thousands of de-chis were passed from the Newmanry to the Testery for breaking by the cryptographers in Room 41. The volume of Lorenz messages from the Germans had gone up sharply and the department within the Testery had to expand correspondingly, remaining like this until the end of the war.

The Testery was now breaking around 90 per cent of the traffic given to them to work on each week. From what I can recall, the pile of unbroken de-chis seldom rose higher than 10 per cent. When we were less busy, we would have a second try on any 'dead ducks' to see whether a second head would have better luck than the one who had tried first. I was fairly sure about my recollection, but I was relieved when I heard Peter Edgerley quote the same figure; he was one of the more serious-minded codebreakers in the Testery. We met a couple of times in London before he died.

The two units, the Testery and Newmanry, had a close working relationship at this point, like two tribes who spoke different languages but lived in harmony together. The Testery moved into a big new building, Block F, which occupied most of the offices in the northern side. The Newmanry occupied the remaining space. We did not have much personal contact with the Newmanry – we did not need to – and the main liaison between the Testery and the Newmanry was Peter Hilton, a mathematician.

The following shows the workload breakdown between the Testery and Newmanry:

Mid 1942 – mid 1943	One to seven stages, all by the Testery	100 per cent by Testery.
July 1943 – February 1944	Five stages, 90 per cent by the Testery	10 per cent by Newmanry (at best).
February 1944 – May 1945	Five stages, 75–80 per cent by the Testery	20–25 per cent by Newmanry.
Overall	75–80 per cent by Testery	20–25 per cent by Newmanry

I have carefully estimated the proportion of the workload attributable to each of the two units. I have also checked my reasoning and figures with Professor Copeland, who fully agrees with them. Overall, the Testery carried out around 78 per cent of the workload and the Newmanry roughly 22 per cent. The bulk of the messages were passed during the last period of the war, 1944–45.

Colossus Mk 1 would have been helpless without the hand breakers in the Testery. The Newmanry needed to know the chi wheel patterns which were supplied by the Testery before Colossus could be used to strip off the first layer of encryption. It wasn't until after D-Day that Colossus Mk 2 started to help the hand breakers out with the chi wheels. But today the balance of the work is not fairly reported. The machines get far more credit than the hand breaking. Breaking Lorenz was a triumph of minds.

The fact is that the Testery could manage everything without the work of the Newmanry, as we had already been used to doing everything before the Newmanry was set up, but the Newmanry could not produce any decrypts without the work of the Testery. Even Shaun Wylie, Peter Hilton and a number of other senior mathematicians in the Newmanry agreed with this when I discussed it with them a few years ago. Without the Testery's manual methods producing the all-important wheel patterns, the Newmanry's machines, however powerful, would not have produced any Lorenz decrypts at all.

I always think that the machines get too much credit in the Newmanry and the hand breakers in the Testery too little. The achievements of the manual method cannot be underestimated, considering the number of vital pieces of signals intelligence gained through the manual process. The Newmanry's task, once they got going, was only to break the chi wheels and to produce the de-chis, which the Testery then had to break. The Newmanry's work was, in effect, a standard run, whereas the challenge facing the Testery was different each day.

Because of Tutte's breakthrough on the Lorenz system, we were able to break 64,000 top-level messages between a handful of senior generals in the German Army, including messages signed by Hitler. We had a 90 per cent break-in rate of all the traffic received in the Testery. These success rates have not been revealed anywhere, and no credit at all was ever given to the codebreakers.

There was a rumour, right at the end of war, that the Newmanry had discovered a way of breaking messages totally by machine, but I never saw any evidence of it. I thought it was highly unlikely; the texts of messages varied so greatly one from another, and machine analysis depends on some element of regularity.

The *General Report on Tunny* was written at Bletchley Park after the war, in 1945, by three codebreakers from the Newmanry – Jack Good, Donald Michie and Geoffrey Timms – but they didn't know much about the work of the Testery. There are only a few lines about it on p.280 of the report:

> The organisation of Major Tester's Section has been described briefly in 14B (c) and more fully in 'Report on Tunny (Major Tester's Section)' and also in the separate report entitled 'History of the Fish Sub Section of the German Military Section'. We do not go into further details here as they are of no great cryptographic interest and are not necessary for the understanding of the present report.

This was sadly how the Testery's work was presented.

Although British Prime Minister Sir Winston Churchill delivered the following speech at the height of the Battle of Britain, it could equally be applied to the men and women of the Testery and the Newmanry:

> Never in the field of human conflict was so much owed by so many to so few.

The country was lucky to have these brilliant people in the right place at the right time to break Lorenz.

12

FROM LORENZ DECRYPTS TO THE WORLD'S FIRST COMPUTER: 1944–45

The first piece of technology used in breaking Lorenz was the British Tunny machine. It was built following the work of Bill Tutte in breaking the Germans' Lorenz SZ40/42 cipher system. The British version was a completely different shape compared to the German box-like structure. It was much bigger, about 6–7ft tall and 4ft wide. It enabled the Testery to do the deciphering job quickly by doing exactly the opposite of what the German twelve-wheel Lorenz machine originally had done. It was like magic. It was staffed by a team of ATS girls in the Testery, who plugged up the day's wheel patterns on the machine, fixed the start points and typed in the cipher text so that the messages could be produced in German clear text.

The machine was designed by Bletchley Park and built by the engineers at Dollis Hill. One of these engineers was Gil Hayward, who visited for a time and repaired the machine in the Testery. It worked well, and shortly afterwards ten or more British Tunny machines were installed for the twenty-four ATS girls to use, eight of them on each shift.

In the meantime, the work of the Newmanry was guided by Tutte's method of first breaking the Lorenz chi wheels. In mid 1943, the Heath Robinson machine (so named after the well-known cartoonist who drew overly complex, machines to achieve simple tasks) was designed to work out the chi wheel patterns instead of having to work them out by hand in the Testery: a very long and laborious job.

The Robinson had two major problems: it was rather slow (the machine only read 2,000 characters per second) and not too reliable. It used two paper tapes which had to be synchronised; one of the tapes would keep breaking from time to time and have to be patiently repaired – indeed, it did look a very unlikely technological break-through. It passed a long paper tape with thousands of letters of cipher text or more through a counter, so that on each of the five lines of impulse, negatives and positives could be counted. Some people in the Testery referred to it sardonically as the 'Flying Bedstead'.

Fortunately, six months after the Robinson started work, in December 1943, an important new machine arrived at Bletchley Park, called Colossus. The name Colossus came from Greek mythology, because of its size – it was about 8ft tall, 15ft wide and 10ft deep at the 'bedstead' end. It almost filled a whole room. The machine had the same function as Robinson – to deduce the chi wheel patterns – but was twice as fast (Colossus scanned 5,000 characters per second). Colossus was designed and built by engineer Tommy Flowers and his colleagues from the GPO.

This invention occurred after a small group of senior codebreakers had briefed Tommy Flowers as to what they needed help with in break-ing Lorenz. These included Max Newman, Bill Tutte and Alan Turing. Tommy Flowers said confidently that he could do it, but it would take him eighteen months to build it – he was told Hitler would have won the war by then. Flowers went away and led his team day and night, added some of his own money to buy the parts needed for the machine and built it at the research laboratory of the GPO at Dollis Hill. In ten months, Colossus was installed at Bletchley Park and was operational after a month or so. It was tested again and again until it worked perfectly.

Colossus Mk 2 was delivered on 1 June 1944, just in time for the Allies to use the intelligence gained to monitor Hitler's plans and ensure the success of the D-Day landings on 6 June 1944. More Colossus machines were built and installed at Bletchley Park to help cope with the rapidly rising volume of Lorenz traffic. Colossus Mk 2 was much more advanced and five times faster than Colossus Mk 1.

It contained 2,400 valves (Colossus 1 had 1,800) and read 25,000 characters per second.

Colossus Mk 2 would greatly speed up the process. It worked out the chi wheel patterns and then removed their influence from the cipher text. This left 'de-chi' messages, which were given to the cryptographers in the Testery for breaking. We would then break a stretch of the cipher text that would be sufficient to allow us to determine the patterns of the other Lorenz wheels – the psi wheels and the motor wheels. A Lorenz message required seven stages to the decode process; after the chi wheel effect had been removed by the Newmanry, there were still five stages to deal with. This involved a lot of manual work for the codebreakers and support staff in the Testery.

After the war, the British Tunny machines, the Robinson machines, the Colossus computers and the rest of war effort machines that had worked alongside were dismantled and recycled for spare parts on the orders of Winston Churchill. However, Government Communications Headquarters (GCHQ) managed to keep two Colossus machines, although they did not give access to anybody else. All the papers we worked on were ordered to be destroyed as well.

HOW LONG DID IT TAKE TO BREAK A MESSAGE BY HAND OR MACHINE?

Many people do not understand just what it was that Colossus did. Many think that Colossus did the whole process, and there is a lot of misunderstanding about how long it took to break a message compared to the hand-breaking method. Some people think Colossus did the whole process of decryption and that there was no need for human codebreakers once Colossus was introduced.

Tony Sale, a volunteer at Bletchley Park, used to say that we usually took four to six days by hand, but other commentators have said that it took nearer to four to six weeks! Neither of these is correct. I have great respect for Tony; he was a remarkable man and a fine engineer.

His great contribution to Bletchley Park was leading his team to reconstruct a Colossus, which you see today in the National Museum of Computing in Block H. For the last few years, when I visited Bletchley Park, we always had a friendly chat and I remember he was always busy standing by his beloved Colossus ready to tell the story to the visitors. I admire his dedication, and he also appreciated what I had been doing for the Park over the years. Tony died in 2011, but he left a fine, lasting legacy: the rebuilt Colossus, which gives great interest and pleasure to thousands of visitors every month. People now come from all over the world to see the Colossus at Bletchley Park.

However, I feel that these remarks gave a misleading impression of the speed with which Lorenz messages were broken. My recollection in the last year of the war was that, with the assistance of the machines, I broke between seven and twelve messages daily and the machine took anything from three to eight hours to produce the de-chi, which was faster than by hand. The machines allowed us to cope with this growth in volume and without them we would have broken much more slowly and fewer messages would have been produced.

I worked on the breaking of messages myself and I know that the majority of them were broken within one shift. It was such an important point that I checked it with Professor Copeland, who confirmed that the majority of messages were broken in two to six hours. If it had taken weeks the message material would have been useless. In fact, the decrypts were treated as red-hot material and quite a lot of them ended up on Churchill's desk possibly even before the German generals received them.

Everybody in the Testery had a different level of skill and knowledge of the German language. We numbered nine codebreakers; some of us had the basic skills, but really only the original three senior codebreakers, of which I was one, did the most difficult job in the team. In the last year of the war, 1944–45, around ten or more new codebreaking personnel were recruited to help cope with the demanding situation in the Testery. They were slower, because they had to learn the 992 combinations by heart and this took a lot of time, but they certainly helped in breaking during the high-volume period.

The biggest advantage of the Colossus machine was to help the Testery in breaking Lorenz much more quickly by identifying the chi wheel patterns faster than could be managed through working them out by hand. This would have been a slower and more laborious process, but still took nowhere near four weeks. I have been concerned for years about the lack of public information about the truth. That is why, at age 87, I started my campaign for better recognition for my colleagues in the Testery. It seems nobody acknowledged what the Testery did, not even Bletchley Park, until recently.

I am the last of the nine cryptanalysts who worked on the actual breaking of Lorenz. Sadly, most of the codebreakers and staff who worked on Lorenz in the Testery died before they could tell their stories, and the Lorenz story is still not fully told because of the high security imposed by the Official Secrets Act. Very few people seem to be aware of Lorenz, Tutte, Tommy Flowers and their achievements. Tommy Flowers was the father of the computer, even though many people appear to think it was an American invention. Even the author of *The Da Vinci Code*, Dan Brown, in his book *Digital Fortress*, claims, 'the computer was invented at Harvard in 1944'.

13

KEY DECRYPTS FROM THE TESTERY AND THEIR IMPACT ON THE SECOND WORLD WAR

The intelligence … from you [Bletchley Park] … has been of priceless value. It has saved thousands of British and American lives and, in no small way, contributed to the speed with which the enemy was routed and eventually forced to surrender … [It was a] very decisive contrition to the Allied war effort.

General Dwight D. Eisenhower

The breaking of Lorenz produced extremely important intelligence which greatly influenced the war in Europe. Lorenz decrypts continued to provide the Allies with vital information. From 1942 onwards, the enciphered messages contained a vital insight into the highest level of German Army High Command, from Hitler's decision to focus on the Russian Front through to the final breakthrough of the Allied armies in spring 1945. The vast majority of the top-level Lorenz traffic was broken in this period and Lorenz decrypts led to the successful conduct of the military operations.

BREAKING 64,000 NAZI TOP-LEVEL MESSAGES

By the end of the war, I calculated that around 64,000 Lorenz messages had been broken by the Testery. Compared with the large volume of Enigma traffic, this is a relatively modest total, but it was gold dust.

It must be remembered that the Lorenz messages contained the highest level of strategic information. I have based my calculation on my own recollection, but also I was able to talk to two ex-members of the Testery who gave me their estimates of how many broken messages were handled each day. One was Helen Currie (née Pollard), who was one of the ATS team taken on in mid 1943. She typed the messages and operated a Lorenz machine. She estimated three messages a day in 1943 and around five messages a day during the Colossus period, when the volume of traffic went up. Helen was the first person to join the Testery for that job and so was more experienced than the others.

I also spoke with wheelsetter Captain Arthur Maddocks. He worked in Room 40 during the period 1944–45 and he gave a slightly higher estimate than Helen. Fortunately, their estimates correspond within 10 per cent of each other. Both had substantial experience in the jobs they were doing at that time. Professor Jack Copeland also agreed with this figure.

I have made a conservative estimate for the number of Lorenz messages we broke in the three-year period which comes out at just above 64,000. Details as below:

Period One – 1 July 1942–30 September 1942 at 40 per week	520
Period Two – 1 October 1942–31 December 1942 at 15 per day	1,170
Period Three – January–June 1943 at 30 per day	4,680
Period Four – July–31 December 1943, twenty-four hours at 72 per day	11,232
Period Five – 1944, with Colossus, twenty-four hours at 112 per day	35,056
Period Six – 1945 (four months) at 112 per day	11,685
Total	64,343

Addressing the crowd! Me at age 11 months, with older brother Arnold, 7. I was born in Wembley, North London.

Aged 10 with my younger brother Frank, 7 (left), and a friend, at Bournemouth seaside in 1930.

Aged 18 with my mother, who had the forethought to arrange for me to spend six weeks in Bad Godesberg in Germany to improve my language before starting my degree course at UCL.

The Mansion. Bletchley Park was owned by Leon family since 1883. From1939 onwards it became the wartime headquarters of the GC&CS for codebreaking and was given the cover name 'Station X'. Our unit, the Testery, was set up in the Mansion in 1941. I was one of the four founding members.

The gate of Black F. From mid-1943 onwards, the Testery (hand breaking) and the Newmanry (machine assistance) settled here until the end of the war.

I was billeted at No. 67 Napier Street during my Bletchley Park days.

Hitler in the headquarters of the Army Group South at the Eastern Front in June 1942, in discussion with his top generals … 'Yes, Hitler, we were listening too!'

Colossus (*above*), the world's first programmable electronic computer, was invented by Post Office engineer Tommy Flowers (*below right*) to speed up the breaking of the chi wheels settings for Lorenz traffic, after Bill Tutte (*opposite*) broke the Germans Lorenz SZ40/42 cipher system. With its twelve encoding wheels, Lorenz (*below*) was vastly more complex than Enigma. Tutte and Flowers' work helped to shorten the war in Europe and brought so much benefit to Britain and to the rest of world. Their achievements were no less than Alan Turing's, and yet most people never heard of them. I called them the 'three heroes' of Bletchley Park.

Bill Tutte was a brilliant mathematician. After the war he returned to Trinity College, Cambridge, and gained a doctorate degree. I remember Bill breaking the Lorenz system in spring 1942 while in the same office as him. 'I saw him staring into the middle distance, twiddling his pencil, and making counts on reams of paper for nearly three months, and I used to wonder whether he was getting anything done. My goodness he was. He had been breaking the Lorenz, without ever having seen the machine! It was painstaking work and an extraordinary feat of the mind.'

Alan Turing, who broke the naval Enigma and probably saved Britain in 1941.

Max Newman. head of the Newmanry, whose machines assisted with the breaking of Lorenz. The unit was set up in mid 1943.

Ralph Tester, head of the Testery, where the Lorenz codes were broken by hand. The unit was set up in 1941.

The Enigma machine, which had three wheels; the cipher was broken by Turing.

Peter Ericsson, a leading codebreaker, linguist and founder member of the Testery. Peter was one of those responsible for the daily breaking of the Lorenz cipher.

Me. I was of the same capabilities, rank and age as Peter Ericsson; we were like twin brothers, but on separate teams. We were both shift leaders in the Testery.

Denis Oswald, ten years older than me, was another founder member of the Testery and leading codebreaker.

Peter Edgerley – a very useful codebreaker in the Testery.

Helen Currie (née Pollard). She was the first ATS girl to operate the British Tunny machine in the Testery.

Peter Hilton, codebreaker and mathematician, worked between the Testery and the Newmanry.

Roy Jenkins started out as a codebreaker but later volunteered to be a wheelsetter. In later life he was a brilliant politician and author.

Bletchley's top brass: Alistair Denniston (*left*) head of the GC&CS since the First World War; Professor Vincent (*centre*), an Italian specialist; and Colonel John Tiltman (*right*) who achieved the first break into Lorenz. But Tiltman couldn't break the system, and it was later passed on to Bill Tutte.

A wartime British 'Tunny machine', used by the ATS girls in the Testery for the last stage of the deciphering process.

TNMOC also houses a rebuilt British Tunny machine.

The rebuild of Colossus exhibition can be seen at TNMOC at Bletchley Park. It was Tony Sale, a fine engineer, who is lead the team that rebuilt the Colossus. It took him thirteen years to complete the work. I feel we owe Tony a large debt of gratitude for this work to bring this exhibit to the public in this museum today.

My first reunion with old colleagues from the Testery since the war. Here I am with Peter and Meg Hilton and my wife Mei, at my London home in Pimlico.

With Tom Colvill and his son Bob, at Ralph Tester's funeral in 1998. We didn't mention Lorenz, as it was still classified.

With Helen Currie, née Pollard, in 2009.

Coming face to face with the Lorenz SZ40/42 for the first time in 2010.

When, in 2008, I realised I was the last survivor among the Lorenz codebreakers, I started giving many talks, with the aim of getting better recognition for my colleagues. I gave a talk at the opening of the Lorenz gallery at TNMOC in 2011 (*right*). Luckily the BBC Wales producer Julian Carey was in the audience.

Julian Carey (*centre*) made a film about for Timewatch. I was pleased to see Tutte and Flowers get recognition they deserved. Julian himself won two BAFTA awards for the best documentary in 2012. He is pictured with John Willis (*left*) and Tim Green (*right*).

Professor Brian Cox with me at the Lorenz gallery at TNMOC for the making of a *Science Britannica* programme in 2012. He took a great interest in Tutte's breaking of Lorenz, which was featured in episode two of the series.

HRH Duke of Kent (*centre*) visited Bletchley Park in 2009 to present veterans with badges. From left to right: Oliver and Sheila Lawn, Judie Hudsdon, Jean Valentine, Ruth Bourne, myself, Simon Greenish and Sir Arthur Bonsall, behind me is Sir Francis Richards.

Date typed 17.9.42.   TUNNY   E.M.(6)

Serial   Time Time of
No   Freq. Ended Origin Date. DEG. Text.
                                      1410/Par. 15.(2)
A942 6530 2052 1452   15/8 528 IBIS meldet unter dem 12/8/42. Laut Meldung vom 11/8 meuteten an AFRIKA Front
                                    1 Indische Panzerbrigade, 10 Mot. Indische Brigade, und 6 Indische Inf. Brigade.
                                    42 Soldaten wurden geschossen, viele Offiziere und Mannschaften eingesperrt.
                                    Alle Radioapparate konfisziert. Teil der Truppen von Front abgezogen. Am 11/8
                                    Flugplatzbelegung EL AMIRIYA (25 Km. südwestl. ALEXANDRIEN). 18 Flugzeuge,
                                    hauptsächlich Kampfflugzeuge, Rest Jagd - Aufklärungs - und Transportflugzeuge
                                    englischer und amerikanischer Herkunft. Sicherung 8 Flak. 5 MG. Batterien, 10
                                    Scheinwerfer, 4 Funkstationen. Vorhanden Bomben und Flugzeugersatzteilmagazine.
                                    Quelle r5m. I Luft. Ob. SUED hat AST im Wehrkreis röm. XVII BBNR 5267/42 geh. röm.
                                    I H. FERNO. Leiter Ast.

An original Lorenz message, ready to be sent on Hut 3 for translation. This was shown to me in 2013. This message was deciphered by my unit in the final stage of the breaking process. (total seven stages). This clear text was in German that I could translate, but my job was to be breaking more codes in the first place.

An example of a break-in showing two Lorenz messages in depth. I can still clearly remember the hand breaking method seventy years later.

I helped to autograph for Bletchley Park on a voluntary basis.

Meeting friends: Dr. Sue Black, a leading campaigner on Saving Bletchley and Phil Le Grand, an editor for the *Bletchley Park Times*, both worked on a voluntary basis.

With Claire Butterfield, who greatly supported the campaign to get recognition for my colleagues. She worked hard as a volunteer with the Bill Tutte Memorial Fund.

As part of the celebrations for Turing's 100th birthday, a group of specialists gave a series of lectures. From left to right, back row: Lord Charles Brocket, Professor Jack Copeland, David Link, Iain Standen, Avi Wigderson, Whitfield Diffie, Martin Campbell-Kelly and John Harper; front row: Mei, me, Margaret Boden and Huma Shah.

Receiving my Honorary Fellowship from UCL in 2013. Left to right: Provost Sir Malcolm Grant, Professor Susanne Kord, me and Professor Jonathan Wolff.

Meeting William Hague. Then Foreign Secretary, he visited Bletchley Park in 2012. His department provided £48,000 of funding to support Bletchley Park's renovation work.

I was interviewed by Nicholas Witchell in 2011, I told him all about the work that I had done on Lorenz, Tutte and Colossus. I was rather surprised when I saw him on BBC News that evening. He got most things right, but he did not say a word about Lorenz – his comments were all about Enigma.

I was presented to HM the Queen in 2011. She took a great interest in Lorenz and asked me a few questions about it, each time with a wonderful smile. A year later I met her again at Buckingham Palace, to my surprise, the Queen said 'I remember you, we met at Bletchley Park.'

The Bill Tutte memorial was finally unveiled in his hometown of Newmarket in September 2014. Bill was never formally recognised during his lifetime, due to the utmost secrecy surrounding Lorenz. Unfortunately, Jerry did not live to see this.

In the early days, there was only one shift, fewer staff and fewer messages. A year later, more staff had been recruited into the department. When the ATS girls worked on the Lorenz machine, we started three shifts within each twenty-four-hour day and we always worked for six days a week. If I had used the figures quoted by my two colleagues, they would have suggested a total nearer to 80,000 messages, but I always prefer to be on the cautious side with such estimates, especially considering how long ago this all happened: memory can play strange tricks over time.

Even 64,000 was a very substantial number of messages. Although it is only a ballpark figure, it shows very clearly what a great quantity of top-level intelligence the messages provided, leading to the success of the Allies and shortening the war – a war which was costing at least 10 million lives a year. A great deal of this succes was due to the fantastic work of Bill Tutte and the Testery.

How did the Lorenz Decrypts Provide Massive Help to the War Effort?

Let us investigate five significant contributions:

1. The Battle of Kursk

In early April 1943, we broke many Lorenz messages in the Testery. I can remember personally breaking messages about Kursk three months before the battle began on 5 July 1943. Through Lorenz decrypts, we at Bletchley knew that Hitler was to move a massive number of troops to the south and we knew fully of the Germans' thinking and planning with the intention of breaking through Russian lines. After their failure at the Battle of Stalingrad at the end of 1942, the Germans were planning another huge assault on the Eastern Front near the city of Kursk, 280 miles south-west of Moscow.

Although the Russians had local information about the German intentions, the main intelligence was provided by the British from Lorenz decrypts. We were able to forewarn the Russians of the attack, tell them when and how the Germans were going to attack and which army groups and tank units were going to be thrown in. We also knew that the Germans planned to use a pincer attack, and told the Russians that the German forces numbered nearly 800,000 men and 2,500 tanks. Everything was in great detail. We were able to warn the Russians three months before the attack was going to be launched, to help them to defend their territory before eventually pushing the Germans back.

A major problem was how to convey the gist of the information to the Russians without letting them know how it had been learned. The British could not tell them about the breaking of Lorenz. At first, they ignored the British intelligence but we managed to find ways to send very many detailed reports to the Russians. We had to disguise it and tell them the information came to us from spies, intimating that we had wonderful teams of spies and other sources of information. In reality, the British intelligence from Bletchley Park was extensive enough to provide the Russians with the whole German order of battle.

Eventually, the Russians put pressure on their factories to deliver as many tanks as possible to the Kursk area. The Russians were able to deliver huge numbers of tanks and to concentrate many divisions of troops on the Eastern Front. The Russians brought together as much as they could, 40 to 50 per cent more than the Germans. Because the Germans had much better quality equipment and super-tanks like the Tiger, the Russians needed greater quantities of armoured vehicles in order to compete.

After many days of bitter fighting, the Red Army managed to repel the German attacks before launching the assault that destroyed the German forces. This led to the greatest tank battle ever – the Battle of Kursk. Fortunately, the Red Army was able to push back the Germans and keep Russian oil supplies intact. In the end, it was a victory for the Red Army. The Russians called it the 'Turning of the Tide'.

The Battle of Stalingrad had been very touch and go for six months during 1942 and early 1943, and Kursk could easily have been just as dangerous for the Allies. If the Russians had lost there they might have been pushed out of the war, losing their oil supplies, and we would have lost one of our most important Allies. Hitler would then have been able to wage the war on the one front, instead of both eastern and western. Luckily, the Russian forces kept the Germans tied up on the Eastern Front, and this helped the successful Allied invasion of Normandy in June 1944 and the final defeat of Nazi Germany in May 1945.

If the Battle of Kursk had been lost, the implications were immense. Germany on the one hand and the Allies on the other would have been in a situation of military stalemate, where neither could have attacked the other successfully, until the atom bomb came along. In fact, Hitler's scientists were working on their own bomb and had brought together 25 per cent of the uranium needed to arm it. It might have been necessary at some point for the Allies to threaten to flatten Düsseldorf or even Berlin just as they flattened Hiroshima a year later.

Most people in Britain are unaware of the Kursk story and its enormous significance, and of the major contribution made by the Lorenz decrypts to its successful outcome. I wonder whether the Russian authorities ever realised the importance of the help that Britain had given. Few people in the world will be aware of the facts of the Lorenz story, which Britain kept secret for more than sixty years after the war. Much of the Lorenz story has remained buried.

2. Before D-Day

Before D-Day, Adolf Hitler had assembled the main body of his troops in the Pas-de-Calais, well north of the Allied landing beaches in Normandy. Hitler thought that the main Allied attack would come in the Calais region. It was crucial for us to know whether the main bulk of the German Army was held in the Calais region (as Hitler wanted) or in the Normandy area (as his generals wanted).

For months before D-Day, using Lorenz decrypts we knew where the Germans expected the Allied attack to come from. The British were very creative as a result and played an extremely clever trick on the Germans. We manufactured various models which, from the air, looked like landing craft and moored them on the coast in Kent and Essex to give the Germans the impression that we were preparing an assault in the Calais region. This meant Normandy was less strongly defended by the Germans than it should have been.

Of course, Hitler never realised we were reading his top-secret messages through Lorenz decrypts. Other sources suggested that 'turned' spies had helped provide the information, but we had the accurate information direct from the Germans' own secret messages via Lorenz.

The German generals didn't fall for the subterfuge – they were professionals – but Hitler did, foolishly in this case. And since Hitler was the boss, he won out. This was, of course, vital information for British intelligence and for the Allied planners before D-Day.

Allied forces landed in Normandy on 6 June 1944. The invasion of Normandy was the largest seaborne invasion to ever take place. On D-Day and in the weeks following the landings, contingents from many nations were involved. The UK, USA, Canada, Free France, Australia, Belgium, Czechoslovakia, Greece, the Netherlands and Poland all played a part. These countries also helped to provide land, sea and air support.

3. After D-Day

Three or four weeks after D-Day, the Lorenz messages continued to give very valuable information. We knew there was a stalemate in Normandy; the Allies were unable to push further south into France and the Germans failed to push the Allies back into the sea. The impasse was broken by an American, General George Patton, who burst through near the Atlantic coast of France. At the same time, General Montgomery also managed to make a breakthrough in the north-east of France.

The German general in charge of their troops was Field Marshall von Kluge. He risked having his forces cut off and surrounded by the Allies; he lost 50,000 of his troops and was taken prisoner by the Allies. Von Kluge's place was taken by his successor, General Model, as they retreated back to their own frontier through Arnhem and beyond.

We broke many Lorenz messages to and from Field Marshall von Kluge during this critical period. Hitler ordered him to go back to Berlin to explain his failure to hold the line, but von Kluge opted to commit suicide rather than face an angry Führer.

4. The Paratroopers Drop

Another important Lorenz contribution occurred during D-Day. In the nick of time, on D-Day itself, further decrypts revealed that a large German Army contingent had moved to where an airborne drop of our troops was planned.

We learned that an extra division had been positioned in an area where the Allies planned to drop the thousands of paratroopers, at a point behind the enemy defence lines in Normandy. A Lorenz decrypt showed that a German infantry division had just been brought up to that area. The men would have been shot to pieces as they slowly drifted down in their parachutes. They were dropped further down the coast by the British in the early morning of D-Day and because of Lorenz intelligence the paratroopers were dropped safely and successfully.

5. The Italian Peninsula

After the British victory of El Alamein, Field Marshal Rommel's troops were forced back along the North African coast. Eventually most of them were withdrawn to Sicily. However, they were pursued further and retreated again to the Italian Peninsula. The Allied forces followed them and sought to drive them out from there too. This, however, proved to be a long and difficult job for the Allied forces, which still included, notably, the 8th Army. The terrain was very hard and mountainous and the German Army put up a stubborn resistance.

Once more, the Allied High Command was very well informed. The Testery again broke many messages to and from Field Marshal Kesselring – the German Army commander in charge of that front – as he beat a fighting retreat up the Italian Peninsula.

D-DAY AT BLETCHLEY PARK

The previous examples are just a few of the many contributions that Lorenz decrypts made to the successful conduct of the war by the Allies on the various battle fronts. We provided vital information that changed the course of the war in Europe and saved tens of millions of lives, crucially in the Allied planning of many major battles, both before and after D-Day. Without the Lorenz messages, had the Allies landed at the wrong place, D-Day could easily have failed and millions of lives would have been lost.

It was in this context that General Eisenhower (later US president) said, quite rightly, after the war that Bletchley decrypts shortened the war by at least two years. This success was down to the achievements of Bill Tutte for breaking the Lorenz cipher system and the Testery for breaking so many of Hitler's top-secret codes. It was the first and perhaps the only war in which one side had such detailed ongoing knowledge of what the other side was planning, thinking and deciding. Lorenz decrypts gave tremendous intelligence to the Allied High Command.

WHAT IF ...?

Many commentators, in talking about Enigma or Lorenz, have tended to focus on the practical details of the system and on the scale and insight of the codebreakers. There has been much less comment about the actual effects of breaking this system. This is the most important aspect of the subject.

The great majority of the British public have been unaware until recently of the massive effect the work at Bletchley Park had on the fortunes of Britain during the Second World War – not just once, but on various occasions. One way of highlighting these achievements is to imagine what would have happened in Britain if these contributions had not occurred.

What if, for instance, Turing had not broken the naval Enigma system in 1941? The answer is classically simple: Britain would have lost the war. We were losing our merchant shipping at a catastrophic rate; the German U-boats were sinking our ships left, right and centre. We were losing, on average, 282,000 tonnes a month before breaking Enigma. If this had continued, Britain would have been starved out in a few months.

What if Bill Tutte hadn't managed to break the Lorenz system, which enabled us to break around 64,000 top-level cipher messages at a 90 per cent rate? Tutte's extraordinary achievement allowed us to read Hitler's intentions and gave insight into his whole military planning and decision-making. Without Lorenz decrypts, the war in Europe would have lasted many more years. This was a war which was costing tens of millions of lives a year.

What if the Russians had failed at the Battle of Kursk? The Nazi army would have broken through and seized the oil resources on which the Russian Army depended. This would almost certainly have knocked Russia out of the war, allowing Hitler to fight on only one front instead of two. Hitler would have been able to put at least twice as many troops into the field against Allied forces on the Western Front. There would probably have been no D-Day landings, as they would have been too risky. The Testery's warnings from the Lorenz decrypts gave the Russians full details of the plans three months before the battle took place and allowed them to deploy the maximum number of tanks and win the Battle of Kursk.

And what if Adolf Hitler had enjoyed a further two more years of power? There were a number of serious possibilities. First, he could have reinforced the defences of his *Festung Europa* (Fortress Europe): he could have made the European mainland impregnable. Second, his scientists were working on their own atomic bomb and had brought together 25 per cent of the uranium they needed for the first A-bomb. Can you imagine Hitler with an atom bomb? It does not bear thinking about. Where would he have threatened first? Europe, including Britain itself, could have faced a Nazi dark age of thirty to fifty years or more.

14

WHY IS SO LITTLE KNOWN ABOUT THE TESTERY?

Why is the work of Bill Tutte and the Testery still largely unknown? The work on Lorenz suffered a longer silence than Enigma. It was revealed sixty-seven years after the war – compared to thirty years for Enigma – having been kept under wraps due to the Official Secrets Act until 2002. Even then, the Lorenz story remained largely unknown to the public and remained untold because many of the Testery people had already died. There was no boost in the media for nearly another ten years. In 1999, there was an excellent programme about the Enigma story called *Station X*. However, there was still no mention of the Lorenz story or the people involved.

Even after declassification, the work of the Newmanry received more publicity than the Testery. There are a number of reasons why the Testery contribution remained unknown. First, after the war, a detailed 500-page report called the 'Tunny Report' – previously ultra-top-secret material – summarised the sequence of the work on Lorenz. It was written by three mathematicians from the Newmanry and so it focused mostly on the Newmanry's mathematical and machinery side, with which they were familiar, but little or nothing about the linguistic side of what went on in the Testery. I have read this report and noted a number of points about the work of the Testery which are not quite accurate. They also did not make adequate comment about the scale of the contribution of the Testery. I do not suggest this was deliberate policy; simply they didn't know the facts about our unit and did not know much about the hand breaking in detail, especially in the first year of breaking Lorenz before the Newmanry came into existence.

Secondly, it is much easier to exhibit the Newmanry's machinery than to show the Testery's hand-breaking work, which consisted of pencil and paper and was destroyed at the end of the war on the orders of Winston Churchill.

Thirdly, at Bletchley Park Museum there was absolutely nothing about the Testery side of the work until 2011, despite my having pressed for it for over five years. Before Lorenz was declassified, there had been a Newmanry exhibit in one of the rooms since the 1990s, plus the display of the replica Colossus machine built by the late Tony Sale in Block H. There was a good deal of space given to the Newmanry's machines and the Enigma, the Bombe and other machinery in general. There was absolutely nothing given to the incredible mental feats of the Testery.

I visited Bletchley Park for the first time since the war in 2007, when I gave a joint talk with Professor Jack Copeland. I realised then that there was nothing about the Testery's work. Ever since, I have suggested an exhibit of the Testery to Simon Greenish (CEO at that time). I provided six boards with texts written by myself and professionally designed with much help from Philip Le Grand, who was the editor of the *Bletchley Park Times* magazine (provided to veterans and members of Bletchley Park). We worked on the boards for a number of months and they were checked by Professor Copeland and Simon Greenish – they both agreed the content. Bletchley Park was ready to have them made and put up, but this did not happen.

Later, I met with Simon a number of times to discuss with him the possibility, and a couple of times Jack joined me when he visited Bletchley Park. Simon was always friendly and supportive, and agreed to put the boards up, but again nothing happened afterwards. I later received polite rejections from him. In 2008 he told me there was no money, and a year later, when I raised the matter again, he said, 'We are too busy at the moment, but we will take it up when we are less busy.' Again, nothing happened.

Then, when the Duke of Kent made his visit to Bletchley Park in July 2009, at my suggestion Kelsey Griffin kindly had the boards made up in A3 size and put up in the Ballroom – a bit small, but they told the Lorenz/Testery story well. After a couple of weeks they were taken down. I could not discover any reason for that and I was quite disappointed. In the next two years, until 2011, I could not mention this subject to Bletchley any more.

Simon Greenish did a great job by helping to resuscitate Bletchley Park over his seven years at the Park, after taking over from Christine Large. Personally, I think we had a good relationship, but I was disappointed by his lack of recognition of the importance of the Lorenz, Tutte and the Testery's work, and his failure to illustrate to the public such an important missing piece of history. On a number of occasions, he had opportunities on TV to mention the Lorenz story but he mentioned Enigma only, even when he was interviewed on the BBC *Antiques Roadshow* programme at Bletchley Park in 2011. I don't blame them too much; perhaps their sights were fixed on raising money and on keeping Bletchley Park going, or perhaps they had not had order and encouragement from GCHQ.

I have felt for some time, at least six years now, that the contribution of the Testery to breaking Lorenz traffic has been greatly undervalued and neglected, not only by the British government but by Bletchley Park itself. People simply did not know anything about the Testery or what it had done. I was not concerned for my own position; I was simply keen to get recognition for the work of my colleagues in the Testery, who did such a fantastic job. Without the Testery breaking all the Lorenz messages, there would have been no need for Colossus or for the Newmanry as a whole. By now, most of the people who worked in the Testery have died and cannot tell the tale so I felt I had a duty to tell the story which is a vital missing piece of history and has been neglected for so long.

If you had visited Bletchley Park previously, you would have seen nothing about Bill Tutte, the Testery or the breaking of Lorenz. No wonder there is so little awareness. Until May 2011 and the opening of the National Museum of Computing at Bletchley Park, there had been limited coverage of the Lorenz story – based just on the information that I had provided. I was glad and very appreciative for that, but even then it only mentioned the Testery briefly. I do hope Bletchley Park from now on can cover a lot more.

The Lorenz story is systematically under-reported. This is why I have campaigned tirelessly for the last six years to raise public awareness of Lorenz – one of the most important breakthroughs of the twentieth century. I think that those in the media have a responsibility to help shed light on this missing piece of history.

15

THREE HEROES OF BLETCHLEY PARK: TURING, TUTTE AND FLOWERS

In 1943, Tommy Flowers and his team designed and built the Colossus which helped the Testery speed up the breaking of Lorenz traffic. This was very urgent – he even put his own money into the project to buy parts for the new machine, which became a great success although nobody could have foreseen what fantastic range of uses would come from this development with modern-day computers. Colossus not only did a wonderful job, but also laid the foundations of the modern world we enjoy today.

Was Flowers rewarded? Well, yes and no. He was given an innovation award of £1,000, but Britain has shown no further recognition whatsoever for his outstanding success. No one at that time thought about how Colossus might be used in the future.

The only people who did celebrate his achievements were those Americans who made a fortune from the computer – Bill Gates and many others. Tommy Flowers made no fortune; his invention of the computer was kept under wraps for decades by the British government. Tommy bitterly wrote:

When, after the war ended, I was told that the secret of Colossus was to be kept indefinitely, I was naturally disappointed. I was in no doubt, once it was a proven success, that Colossus was a historic breakthrough and that publication would have made my name in scientific and engineering circles – a conviction confirmed by the reception accorded to ENIAC, the US equivalent made public just after the war ended. I had to endure all the acclaim given to that enterprise without being able to disclose that I had anticipated it.

(Quoted in Jack Copeland, *Colossus*, p.82)

To the question of which of the three heroes at Bletchley Park had the greatest impact, I would answer that you can't really extol one more than the others. The truth is that each could not have achieved what they did without the other. It is important to remember that if the breaking of Lorenz had not been so vital and if Bill Tutte had not managed to work out the Lorenz system, we would probably never have heard of Tommy Flowers or the Newmanry. There would have been no need for them. Colossus was built for one purpose only – to help the Testery break Lorenz traffic more quickly.

It is important to remember that codebreaking at Bletchley Park was a team effort. Without the other team members, we would not have achieved what we did. However, some people contributed more than others. Tutte's achievement has been described by some as the outstanding mental feat of the twentieth century. Tutte had never ever seen the machine; it took him nearly three months to break the whole system, using mathematics and strict logic. It was certainly not, as one commentator called it, 'relying on instinct and lucky guesses'. Lorenz should never, ever, have been broken, and certainly no one should be able to break such a system by guesses!

Tutte described his methods of breaking Lorenz in full detail in his chapter in the *Colossus* book – there were no lucky guesses there. I was working in the same office as Bill Tutte when he was breaking the Lorenz system in spring 1942 and I saw his endless patience and persistence. Because of Tutte's breakthrough, we were able to break around 64,000 of the top-level messages and 90 per cent of all the traffic in the Testery. The work of Tutte and the Testery seems to have been deliberately played down.

Tutte and Flowers both suffered heavily in silence for so long after the war. Turing continued working on his computing projects, taught in the foundation of maths, artificial intelligence and so on. Turing's homosexuality was considered a security risk at the time since it was suspected that his contacts in other countries might include a spy, and therefore there was a risk of him leaking secret information. Homosexual acts were not legal in the UK at that time. As a result of a criminal prosecution in 1952, he accepted treatment with female hormones rather than go to prison. He died in 1954, aged just 42; some believe he was in a state of depression and committed suicide.

Bill Tutte preserved the secrecy of his work, just as many others did. Tutte emigrated to Canada in 1948 and worked at the University of Toronto where he pursued a fine career and took a professorship. He was made a Fellow of the Canadian Royal Society and later was recognised by the prestigious Royal Society in Britain, which made him a Fellow (for his other successful work) which I regard as probably the highest accolade in this country. But none of those achievements compared to his wartime contribution. Tutte's achievement of working out all the twelve wheel patterns by logical inference was a staggering achievement – almost a miracle. He was credited with shortening the war in Europe by two years, saving countless lives, but he received no official recognition or public acclaim for it by his own country, even to this day. From the Honours Committee he received neither honour nor award – absolutely nothing. Tutte died in 2002 aged 85 and is buried in Canada.

THREE HEROES REWARDED?

In the early nineteenth century, Wellington defeated Napoleon Bonaparte at the Battle of Waterloo. A grateful nation rewarded him with a large and handsome house, now known as No. 1 Piccadilly, in London, and awarded him a dukedom. A century earlier, after the Seven Year War, John Churchill, ancestor of Sir Winston Churchill, also well regarded by the nation, was awarded an even more grandiose property – Blenheim Palace and its substantial grounds. He was also created the Duke of Marlborough.

In 1941, Alan Turing also served the nation by breaking the naval Enigma and therefore stopping the German U-boats sinking so many convoy supply ships – indeed he saved the country. Was he rewarded? Well, again, yes and no. He was awarded a bonus of £200 pounds and given an OBE. I don't feel this is much for saving a country; ordinary senior civil servants are often given an OBE. The government had a great opportunity to remedy this enormous deficiency when 2012 was named 'Alan Turing Year'. Turing saved the nation from a Nazi dark age, which is constantly underplayed. The government, in my opinion, treated him shabbily.

In 1943, Tommy Flowers did a remarkable thing. He was an extraordinary man. The next time you use your computer, games console, smartphone, etc., spare a thought for Tommy. He was treated slightly better than Turing, receiving an inventor's award of £1,000. Still, not a lot for what he did and peanuts compared with today's sportsmen and pop stars.

Turing and Flowers were lucky; Bill Tutte got nothing. No wonder he went off to Canada after the war. Eventually he was made a top-ranking Fellow of the Royal Society in both Canada and Britain. This, of course, is a most prestigious honour. Tutte's wonderful wartime work which benefited the country so substantially has been given not a single honour.

Bill Tutte was the least well known of the three heroes at Bletchley Park. I have been struggling for the last six years to improve the situation and may have made some progress with the Lorenz story and some recognition for Bill Tutte, as a result of the BBC *Timewatch* programme. I have frequently given talks, written articles and given interviews, especially regarding Tutte's achievements, as I had my own personal experience of actually being with him when breaking the Lorenz traffic.

Luckily, one day in May 2011, on the opening day of the National Museum of Computing, I inspired Julian Carey, who had heard me give a talk at Bletchley Park. Julian, a BBC producer in Cardiff, was interested and soon after contacted me and promised to make a film about the Lorenz story. He was as good as his word. This programme was entitled 'Codebreakers: Bletchley Park's Lost Heroes' and has been shown on BBC2 four times since October 2011. This helped greatly to spread the word about the Lorenz story and I am truly grateful to him for that. I am so glad that Tutte and Flowers got full credit in this programme.

One of the welcome side effects of the film was to make the people of Newmarket, Tutte's hometown, realise that they had an unsung hero on their doorstep. In 2013, the good folk of Newmarket clubbed together to fund a memorial in honour of their town's hero. The Bill Tutte Memorial Working Group secretary, Richard Fletcher, told me the memorial will cost around £150,000. They have been pledged £100,000 so far and it will be ready by June 2014, I have been invited to its unveiling and hope to attend. At the time of writing, so far as I know, the government have made no contribution to it. Newmarket deserves all the support we can give. Their website is listed at the end of this book.

There is very little public celebration of these three men. The year 2012 was the centenary anniversary of Turing's birth, but the celebration did not seem to me to focus enough on the real benefit that his work brought to his country. There was no support from official bodies. There had been a long campaign for years to clear Turing's name of his criminal offence. (Turing was persecuted for having a sexual relationship with another man and for threatening the security of Great Britain.) Before Christmas in 2013, I was pleased to hear that the Queen had granted a posthumous pardon to Alan Turing, fifty-nine years after his death. He died – it is thought that he killed himself with cyanide – in 1954. He was one of three heroes at Bletchley Park, a brilliant mathematician and codebreaker.

Turing's supporters proposed that his head be printed on the £10 note, but this was rejected. A friend of mine put forward the case to the Honours Committee and I do remember signing an e-petition for it recently, but this was rejected too. The reason given by the committee was that Turing was dead, so he could not posthumously be given an honour.

We could not talk about Tutte's or Flowers' achievements for decades after the war. Tutte died in 2002 – the year that Lorenz was finally declassified. Tommy Flowers, who developed Tutte's idea and designed and built the Colossus, died in 1998 having received no public recognition for his achievements.

You can see the General Montgomery statue in White Hall, but where can you see any statue of our heroes? The cryptographers did something more extraordinary, and I would be happy to see statues of these three heroes in Trafalgar Square. I think any one of them is in the class of the Duke of Wellington or the Duke of Marlborough, perhaps more so. The effect of what they did was enormous. Without these three great minds and the many other supporting personnel at Bletchley Park, Britain and the rest of Europe would be a very different place today. Britain was lucky to have these brilliant men in the right place at the right time.

The three heroes did not, of course, do their work for any reward; they did it because it urgently needed to be done. I have been seeking better recognition for Bill Tutte's success since 2007, because it seemed no one had heard of his name. Raising the subject was not easy and it was hard without media support. For the last couple of years, things have improved, especially after Her Majesty the Queen and the Duke of Edinburgh visited Bletchley Park and after the BBC *Timewatch* programme featured the story.

Though I am feeling my age, I shall continue to work for my colleagues' recognition. My goal, in the years left to me, is to try to get better recognition for Tunny, the Testery and for the three heroes, Tutte, Turing and Flowers. After all, I am only 93 ...

PART THREE

AFTER THE WAR

16

THE WAR CRIMES INVESTIGATION UNIT: 1945-47

After the war, I was sent by the Foreign Office to Europe for another important job, while many people still had to wait at Bletchley for new jobs. I was a member of the War Crimes Investigation Unit in Europe for two years from 1945 to 1947.

In May 1945, the immediate need for large numbers of cryptographers ceased to exist, and I was assigned to just about one of the most different jobs in the army it was possible to conceive. I was sent to Bad Oeynhausen, in the British Zone of Occupied Germany. This was a medium-sized town and the headquarters of the British forces were there. I was to report to Colonel Nightingale, head of the War Crimes Investigation Unit. My task was to travel to different parts of Europe to interview witnesses and victims in various war cases, taking legal statements from them for use in court, to help bring Nazi criminals to trial; it allowed me to continue to use my German and French.

This unit was made up of officers who were given a car and army chauffeur so they could go anywhere to interview witnesses of war crimes and sometimes the suspected perpetrators of the crimes. Naturally, we spent most of our time on the road, driving about and moving from one case to another. It took time to bring the cases together, but we never got to see the results of our efforts and so we were left with a rather empty feeling. I found the time spent driving very boring. It may have been an exciting job for other officers, but it wasn't for me. I am just being honest, not negative, about my experience for those two years. It was just very different from the constant pressure of life and work at Bletchley Park, especially after the very busy, important and exciting four years' codebreaking.

First of all, I had to learn to drive a car. I was taken out by a fellow officer, Major Thornton, for my first lesson. The machine I was given to learn on was a Jeep; getting it into first or second gear involved a masterpiece of timing. For a whole day, I drove (or rather, did not drive) the Jeep, crashing the gears every time I tried to put the car in motion. The patience of Major Thornton became extremely fragile, but he held it – just. Deep into the second day, luckily the penny dropped and I had no further difficulty. I finally got the hang of it and in a short space of time became a competent driver. Those two days, however, remain the most embarrassing, humiliating and stultifying of my life. Thereafter, the vehicles we used were ex-German Army saloon cars made by Mercedes Benz – steady, sturdy workhorses. They were not automatics, but the gears were perfectly manageable, and I drove them, eventually, for many thousands of miles.

I was coping well with the new experiences presented by the War Crimes Investigation Unit in terms both of doing the work and running a team of people, but I felt like I had been put back into kindergarten – I had to deal with many new challenges. I was to travel a great deal instead of being fixed to one location, and rather than working within the same group day by day I was to be brought into contact with a multiplicity of different people. Instead of wrestling with problems on paper I had to deal with problems involving people. All of my prior training had not equipped me for being a kind of travelling detective. Before Bletchley Park, there had at least been the six weeks at Bedford training for codebreaking. Here, there was nothing, with one exception – to do the job at all I had to be able to drive and look after a car and my chauffeur, with whom I shared the driving fifty–fifty.

The task called for someone trained as a detective, able to seize the few facts presented to him in a short briefing document and, in the case of witnesses, to put flesh to the bones – but reliable flesh, for the statement might later be used in court. Legal training would have been desirable, but few of us had that. An underlying toughness and the ability to challenge the witnesses' assertions without losing their willingness to co-operate were also very necessary. This was like walking a very difficult tightrope, and in German, too, or French. The job was made harder by the fact that I was never given more than one witness to interview for any one case, so that one could never accumulate evidence or cross-check one story against another. This was partly because witnesses and the accused in a given case were often scattered over the face of Europe so interviews had to be grouped geographically, rather than by case. Therefore, one investigator might find himself interviewing for a number of different cases in a given area.

At Bletchley Park there had almost always been a sense of achievement – on most days, in fact. At War Crimes, it was much more difficult to judge how well one was performing. The job was an important one, bringing justice to individuals accused of horrendous crimes, and there was a vast amount to do after the war. These were not just the headline criminals – Himmler, for instance – but many others accused of crimes against individuals. I worked hard and probably turned in an adequate performance, but I would not claim more than that. It was one of the few periods of my life which I did not enjoy. In reality, I would say the CV-shufflers at the War Office had chosen the right man with the language skills for this type of job, but I didn't enjoy it.

There were others in the unit who were better suited to the work and more extrovert than I, with a real flair for the effective pursuit of war criminals. They often had a greater personal incentive – they had lost friends or relatives at the hands of war criminals and they had a massive desire to even up the score.

My work mostly proceeded steadily on an even keel. It was quite hard, with a great deal of car travel, and the time spent at the HQ of the War Crimes Investigation Unit in Bad Oeynhausen, or in the mess there, was very limited. I did not get to know fellow officers well as there was no time to do so. Of course, I could not speak at all about what I had been doing at Bletchley Park up to this point.

While I felt I had probably performed excellently during my time at Bletchley Park, my period at the War Crimes Investigation Unit seemed much less rewarding. Building an effective case against a suspected war criminal was a difficult task, given that victims, perpetrators and witnesses were by now mostly scattered over Europe. I was never called upon at the arrest of anyone or to give testimony in court. I ended up feeling that other officers had probably had quite different experiences from me, in spite of all my efforts, though I feel I did quite well for what they needed. However, the law operates very slowly, especially when a case involves different countries, and it may be that some of our cases led eventually to trials in later years – in my case, after I was demobbed.

I suppose everyone in their lifetime has several episodes to recall which make their toes curl in embarrassment or shame. One such occurred to me when I visited Bonn, near Cologne on the River Rhine, in search of a witness. I attended a meeting in the town hall in Bonn where people applied for permits and benefits. I must have been slightly higher above the petitioners because I recollect a small sea of people, some with faces upturned. By an extraordinary coincidence, I saw Frau Becker, the landlady of the boarding house where I had spent six weeks at the age of 18 to improve my German (see Chapter 2). She was obviously trying to catch my attention to ask for my help for some reason.

I went down to look for her, but there was such a huge mob that I was unable to find her. To this day, I regret not being able to find her. She was probably trying to get a permit to do something or other; you needed a permit for everything at that time. Frau Becker had been a decent *hausfrau* (housewife), hardworking and respectable. She was non-political and, whatever the delicacy of intervening in her case (one cannot really appreciate now the awkwardness of impinging on other officers' areas of responsibility in the army), I should at least have tried to find out what her needs were. My toes today are still unconvinced – and still curl. If I had been able to speak up for her it could have helped her a great deal. I was a full uniformed officer and that carried a lot of weight.

My demobilisation, when it came in May 1947, was not unwelcome. However, I faced a very uncertain future when I returned to London.

17

TRANSLATING A BOOK FROM FRENCH IN 1947

One of the cases that I dealt with in the War Crimes Investigation Unit was that of Madame N. Hélène Jeanty, a brave Belgian lady who, with her family, lived in Brussels during the war. The Gestapo had picked up her husband. She had kept a diary of the events and was looking for somebody to translate it from French into English. She had a publisher interested – Sheppard Press in London.

Although I had never formally translated a book before, I was 27 years old then and she knew my French was good. My French had become fluent and I felt confident that I could do a good job on it. I was happy to offer my services and Sheppard Press accepted. The book was titled *Certified Sane*. It was a hardback book about 235 pages long and priced at 12s 6d. Sheppard Press paid me £200 in 1948 – not a lot by today's standards, but quite a good fee for those days: you could buy half a house with it.

The Jeantys were one of those very brave families who formed part of a chain of safe houses to help British airmen who had been shot down over Europe to return to Britain, where most of them took up flying again. The family had a special hidey-hole constructed and were successful for a number of months. One day at 6 a.m., however, the dreaded knock on the door came. The Gestapo entered and searched the house from top to bottom, but did not find the hidey-hole. Finally, after a very tense time, they left to great relief all around.

However, an hour later the Gestapo came back – it was a trap. They found a hidden airman and took him prisoner. They seized Monsieur Jeanty, and his wife never saw him again.

I was very glad to help bring this courageous woman's story to the British public. The translation went ahead and had a very successful publication. The book was well received. As a result, I later learned that it had not only been published by Sheppard Press; it was published again by another firm in a glossier version, but with the same translation. The translation had taken me about three months altogether. It was much harder work than one imagines and quite demanding.

MY LIFE HAS BEEN MORE LIKE A LEAF ON A STREAM

By now, I had started wondering what I should do next.

Some people have the general direction of their lives plotted out for them at an early age, as did one of my colleagues at Bletchley Park in 1944: Captain Roy Jenkins. His father was a prominent Labour MP and even during the Bletchley Park days it was clear what direction Roy's life would take, and superbly successfully he followed it. I don't know how he got into my team in the Testery at Bletchley Park. We cryptographers in Room 41 all had a constant need to use German, but Roy did not have any. After three months, he found it difficult to deal with the codebreaking job and he had to withdraw himself to a much easier job in wheel setting where German was not essential. After the war, he took up his political career following in his father's footsteps, and that suited him very well and he proved highly successful. My life has been more like a leaf on a stream: it has moved along with the current, bumping into objects on the way, but mainly proceeded serenely with the current. There has been no master plan, but a series of lucky accidents. At age 93, now, when I look back, I feel reasonably happy that my life has been useful, enjoyable and successful overall.

I was originally intended for the Foreign Office. By that point, I had used my German for six years and French for two, both eventually fluently. I had a qualification. I took easily to languages, so I had opted to study German and French for my degree at UCL from 1939 to 1941. After the war I applied for the Foreign Office rather half-heartedly a couple of times, but there were no vacancies. I applied for another couple of advertised jobs, but I lacked any sense of real direction. I was again gliding gently down the stream.

My father was a senior bank clerk in the head office of Lloyds. My elder brother, Arnold, was already in one of Lloyds' branch offices in Wembley. A good, solid, highly respectable job in the Foreign Office was clearly the right ticket for me and the same could be said if I was to take a job in Lloyds. But I had no desire to join Lloyds Bank, in which both my father and brother spent forty years of their careers.

I had been exiled to Aberystwyth in Wales for my university days and only had a few contacts still alive, none of them useful for job-seeking. I could not tell potential employers what I had been doing during my time spent in the army at Bletchley Park. The mention of Bletchley now conveys something to many informed people, but at that time it would have meant nothing – even if one had been allowed to mention it.

I was snatched away from Bletchley Park quite suddenly and did not have the time or the nous to establish contacts with the few people I had known and liked there. Many went back to Oxford to teach or to continue their studies or found jobs somewhere else, but I had no contact for a job at that time. Others, such as Peter Ericsson, disappeared – maybe drifted into some other army assignment – and I never saw them again.

My two-year absence in Germany effectively broke the few links I had with Bletchley Park people. In the War Crimes Investigation Unit, it was almost impossible to nurture relationships as we were dispatched to a new assignment a day or two after getting back to HQ in Bad Oeynhausen. One seldom saw the same faces twice. I was not working on things I enjoyed and altogether it was a fairly bleak prospect that faced me by mid 1947. When I got back to the UK, I was unemployed for the only time in my life.

To get a good job, one requirement is a list of good contacts or a sound professional qualification to pursue a career as a lawyer, a surveyor, an architect, etc. Another is a predestined target, such as my earlier half-formed plan to go for the Foreign Office. It is helpful to have parents and other relatives in a good position or just sheer luck. But I did not have any of these and I was not allowed to talk about my secret job at Bletchley Park or WCIU for years – in fact, for more than sixty years after the war.

I was not one of those who collected addresses or phone numbers when moving on from one activity to the next and my contacts were very limited as I was still young. Not, I would think, your average life history – each main switch of direction was semi-accidental, rather than planned. The stream, in the shape of Adolf Hitler, had swept me along a quite different channel.

18

FIFTY YEARS OF MARKET RESEARCH: 1948-98

INTRODUCTION TO CPV, AN INTERNATIONAL MARKETING RESEARCH COMPANY

In 1948, after I got back to Britain from the War Crimes Investigation Unit, I tried to get a position in the Foreign Office. While I had been away for two years in Europe, the vacancies had aa been filled. I waited and waited; I tried again after a couple of months but I had no luck. Because I had signed the Official Secrets Act at Bletchley Park, I was not able to tell anyone about my wartime work. This was a considerable limitation for finding a job, so I had to look elsewhere. I tried for a number of jobs I felt I was suited for, but was not accepted.

One day, I met a person in the street in London whom I recognised as someone I had seen at Bletchley. I had not known her well as she worked in a different department. She was Carole Beddington and we arranged to have lunch together, to talk, ever so discreetly, about old times. In the course of it, she asked me what I was doing and I replied, 'Very little.' She, at least, had some idea that I had carried some weight at Bletchley Park and she offered to get me an introduction to international advertising agency CPV (Colman, Prentis & Varley – the names of the three founders).

Her father, Jack Beddington, was a board director of CPV, a medium-sized but flourishing advertising agency in London. He was the director in charge of the creative side of the agency. In a few days, I went along to meet her father, I was interviewed by him at 34 Grosvenor Street W1, in Mayfair, the international headquarters. A man aged around 55 and slightly corpulent, he wore a large red cummerbund which concealed a good deal of the excess weight. In twenty minutes he evaluated me as clearly not an advertising man, a good deal more accurately than the War Office had. It seemed that I was not to be regarded as God's gift to advertising.

However, they had a market research company, so I was very politely redirected to the company's market research firm called Market Information Services Limited (MIS), set up by the advertising agency to help its clients in the analysis of their marketing problems. I was given an introduction to Harry Henry, 38 years old, the managing director of MIS. Luckily, Harry took me on as a trainee research executive. I was very pleased to have landed safely.

By now it was 1949, and I started the job with Harry Henry at 1 Old Burlington Street, in Mayfair. Market research was a new and developing profession at the time. A number of other companies had sprung up, many of them set up by advertising agencies to help their clients learn more about their market and help make advertising budgets much more effective. It was really excellent training and much more interesting than working for a client company, where one might deal only with one product. I began my new career in market research and marketing, which lasted for fifty years. I thoroughly enjoyed it and I was quite successful. Later on I even set up two of my own companies and during these years I can never remember having a day of boredom.

I was very grateful for the introduction by Carole Beddington which worked out so well and I wrote a warm letter of thanks. However, I received no reply from her and in those days relatively few people had a private telephone, so I was not able to make contact nor thank her personally. The introduction brought me not only a job but a career, and I am still immensely grateful to her for doing me such a favour.

By this haphazard and rather fortuitous event the direction for the rest of my life was set. A life, for me, full of interest and variety

– adventure even – in the field of market research, combined in the later years with marketing. The irony in this, of course, is that my qualifications in languages and six years of army service played no part in me being accepted for the job: a classic case of 'it's not what you know, but who you know'.

MIS was a good company, handling a variety of products and services and I was fortunate to have joined them. Harry Henry was an intelligent researcher with a flexible mind and strong character, and was able to analyse the problem the client brought to him and work out how to resolve it. It was a pretty new profession and I had had no previous contact with it. There was everything to learn. In the next six years I worked hard and learned fast from Harry Henry. It took me two or three years to be fully trained.

By the early 1950s, I was one of the two senior research executives working directly under Harry Henry. The other was Leonard Smith, a mathematician. I was good with sums and comfortable with numbers but had not taken them to degree level as he had. My contribution was a sound common sense (that uncommon commodity) that helped me to analyse the marketing problems and to evolve the market research solution. The need for mathematics only arose if there was a difficult sampling problem or in calculating sampling error. Such specialist needs were in fact very rare. MIS provided a wonderful and continuous training in most forms of research – except for the so-called qualitative research that I was to specialise in later.

In 1954, after six years working at MIS, my career took a sudden and totally unexpected turn. One day I was called over to the main agency, CPV, to see the director in charge of their whole overseas operation, Leslie Cort. He laid out an exciting and terrifying proposition before me: CPV had an important branch agency in Caracas, Venezuela, with a range of clients for whom it worked in a number of markets overseas. The agency had a need for market research for some of these clients, including Shell Oil, to look at attitudes towards the company and its major competition, Esso Oil, and to look at the situation in their markets. A large proportion of Shell's production came from the oilfields in Venezuela. The country was ruled by a military dictator General Pérez Jiménez until 1957. CPV wanted someone there to establish a research unit to help the agency service of this important client. Would I be interested?

I had of course no Spanish, but Leslie Cort knew I had fluent French and German, so acquiring Spanish ought to be relatively easy. While a fascinating opportunity, it was nonetheless pretty daunting for a young man such as I at that time. The attitude towards travel then was, of course, totally different from that of today: a visit to Paris was a venture, to Italy even more so. Nowadays, people – especially the young, take such trips in their stride. To work in Venezuela was then very exciting; I took the risk and accepted the job.

The company I set up, DATOS ('Facts' in Spanish), was the first ever market research company in South America in 1954. It still exists, a much larger company with more than 300 people now. At the time I worked in Venezuela the country was a real honeypot, attracting people from a wide range of countries to take advantage of the great opportunities it offered, including very high salaries. It also had an attractive climate and Caracas itself had all the modern conveniences. The city of Caracas was quite large, and levels of car ownership were high. As a result, the population was very mixed and a number of countries were represented among senior staff of DATOS.

In the early months, I had to work very hard with DATOS. Everything had to be done from scratch. There were no facts on which to base samples; there was no social class structures to provide that essential element of analysis; there were no frameworks for sampling; there were no trained interviewers; and there were no staff to handle the results. Above all there were no clients. In both cases there were ample reasons to feel that the cause of the future could be a failure; but within a year or two, I had built up a substantial network of clients and the future looked comfortable.

CORPA was an adverting agency in Caracas. CPV had bought a one-third share in CORPA. Leslie Cort from CPV in London, sent out Steve Jennings to run the company. Steve's achievement was itself quite remarkable. He ran a veritable League of Nations – no two department heads came from the same country. Leslie Cort has a lot of credit due to him for having picked Steve and myself, two young executives, and thrust us into managerial positions 5,000 miles away in Venezuela with a completely different culture. We were both very successful and became best friends.

During my time in Venezuela, the cost of living was high; most items cost twice as much as in the UK. However, salaries were often more than twice as high so compensating for this and it was possible to live very comfortably and save some money for a rainy day.

Life in Venezuela was very enjoyable, but during 1959, it became apparent I had done all that I could at DATOS, and after five years I decide to leave. DATOS had 35 staff by then, which was quite a good size for a small country like Venezuela. Of course, I needed a new person to take over my job as managing director, which was another quality Englishman, Andrew Templeton. I had no hesitation in offering him a position to replace me.

I was invited to go to New York to represent the international organisation CPV and sell services to potential American clients. I made a substantial number of contacts in that year. I returned to MIS in London and was appointed as a board director of the company. Within a few years I became the managing director, responsible for everything, including UK clients as well as overseas. Here I stayed for the next ten years. I had a good salary and a good position in the company, but life began to lack challenge and excitement, I found it uninspiring. This was the one of the few times in my whole work experience where I really did not have great enthusiasm for what I was doing. It was an uncomfortable feeling. In fact it was a good time for me to rethink my future. I looked back at everything I had done – quite a lot of successful things: I had mostly been in top positions in each of my past jobs. I had done a good job in setting up and running DATOS for five years. I had been a senior research executive in MIS in the early days, the managing director for the last ten, and I had run my department in the Testery at Bletchley Park very successfully for four years during the Second World War. I felt I had the confidence to do more; I came up with a different idea.

In the early 1970s, I decided that much as I loved CPV, MIS and the people in them, the time had come for me to strike out on my own. It was a very exciting prospect. I thought I had a wealth of experiences, a wide arrange of clients in the UK and in Europe. I had established a good reputation in the market research area. I had a particularly good relationship with the research manager Fred Johnson at British Gas, who was very experienced, technically very sound and friendly. One day, when I mentioned to Fred that I was planning to set up my own company, rather to my agreeable surprise, he told me that he had every confidence in me and he would give some work to me if I set up independently. This was a further help: it gave me the opportunity and confidence to set out with my own company. While a strong motivation would have been the benefit of success, it also has the risk of failure lurking very much in the background. However, I thought it was an adventure with some possible success, and I decided to go ahead with the idea.

My first company, operating in the UK, was called Roberts Research Limited. After a year or so, I set up a second, Euroresearch Limited, which was a pioneer in offering multi-country studies across Europe. There was no one offering general market research in a similar way at that time. In this way, I was able to make full use of my languages – German, French and Spanish – in my work. I provided a high-quality service to my clients and the businesses grew steadily year after year. I never had a year in which I made a loss and I never failed an employee. But, as ever, running two businesses meant hard work and a lot of responsibilities.

In 1993, NOP (National Opinion Polls) – the second largest market research company in the UK at that time – approached me. Ivor Stocker, one of the managing directors, made an offer for both of my companies and offered me five years as a consultant to NOP. By now, I had reached the dizzy age of 73, I had done enough for England and it seemed a suitable moment to retire. I was happy passing on my major clients to NOP. I found myself for the next five years doing almost as much work as I was doing before, finding that I enjoyed it more than ever, because this time I was without all the responsibilities of running the finances and personnel of my two companies.

For fifty solid years, my family's welfare was dependent on my ability to achieve success in my work. I had huge responsibilities. Luckily, I was able to make enough money to ensure the family had enough to spend on their everyday lives – pay for the bills, schooling, university, holidays, whatever was needed. But to achieve this success called for constant hard work and long hours. I regretted that I could not spend more time with my family but there was no alternative.

Overall, I thoroughly enjoyed my fifty years working in market research. I was very lucky to have fallen by accident into this profession. I loved the work I was doing and was prepared to give a lot of time to it. I loved writing reports – of which I wrote many – I loved dealing with the clients and I loved creating solutions and problem-solving.

Looking back over the years of my work and my life, when I first went to Bletchley Park the future was bright. I was young and single, without any worries in the world, no responsibilities for a family. On the family side, I had not enjoyed the same success as at work. I was too focused on my work and did not choose wives who could cope with that and provide the support I needed. I do not say this as a criticism; I was a bit under-developed on that side and knew little about that mysterious body of people called women. However, third time lucky.

On the career side, however, I always worked hard and I had the capacity to handle the work I loved and enjoyed, in cryptography or anything else. When I went out to Venezuela, the odds were all against me succeeding. None of the conditions needed to set up a market research company was in place. It was really hard, in a country where I didn't speak the language, and I was not sure of the future. Nor could I guess how my own companies in the UK would turn a loss or gain.

The leaf had travelled a long way down the stream, but so far had arrived safely.

PART FOUR

SEEKING RECOGNITION FOR TUTTE AND THE TESTERY

19

MY SIX-YEAR CAMPAIGN

I have strived to bring the Lorenz story to the attention of the public since 2007 when nobody had heard of it. I wanted to obtain better recognition for my colleagues, in particular Bill Tutte and Tommy Flowers. Their level of success must be almost unprecedented in the history of cryptography, particularly for such high-quality intelligence. I had hoped that a Lorenz/Testery exhibition could be developed, because there was a lack of awareness of it outside of Bletchley Park and there had been no support in the media.

I had to fight tooth and nail for the first few years, but the effort also greatly enriched my late 80s and early 90s. I am in a hurry. I am not getting any younger and the effort involved has been extremely hard on me. I have been struggling to get a proper Lorenz exhibition at Bletchley Park itself and I had difficulty in getting people interested in making a television programme about the fascinating story in the earlier days of my campaign.

I tried a series of initiatives and contacted several media outlets. I placed the story on the internet and invited the media to contact me, but I got precisely nowhere and made very little progress in the first four years between 2007 and 2011. I was the only man with the road map to the eventual destination and the road has been long and tough. It has been a hard journey and very challenging. I never knew whether I would succeed or fail, but it was a constant source of interest and I felt a strong sense of duty. I did not have the opportunity to begin my quest earlier, as I would have liked, because the story had not been declassified at that time.

Why is it so important to me to do this? The main reason is that Lorenz decrypts had a major influence on the course of the war and this has not been recorded well and has been largely overlooked so far. Because the highest level of secrecy was preserved around Lorenz for so long, sadly, none of my fellow codebreakers in the Testery are still alive today. I am the last surviving codebreaker to have worked on Lorenz. I regard myself as being very lucky, at my frail old age, to be able to impart the inside story. It is an important piece of missing history, and I should, and can, tell it.

My plan to help educate the public on this truly mammoth undertaking was to give talks, write articles, give interviews and raise awareness in any other ways that I could conceive. But the number of people reached publicly remained small and the venues were scattered. I gave talks at universities, government bodies, Google, Winchester and Warminster, Cheltenham Festival, Cambridge University, a number of schools in different areas and of course at Bletchley Park itself. The audiences varied in size from 1,200 right down to nine.

All of these efforts were unpaid. My objective, of course, was not to make money but to spread the word about Tutte and Lorenz. After many of my talks I received a lot of public support. The response to my talks was invariably positive; people shared my views and strongly agreed that the story deserved greater recognition.

The situation improved significantly when Her Majesty the Queen paid a visit to Bletchley Park in mid 2011. I was formally presented to Her Majesty and the Duke of Edinburgh, with all the publicity that it generated in the media. I was featured in newspapers and on radio and interviewed about this vital piece of missing history and 'one of the most important breakthroughs of the twentieth century'. Without the coverage in the media, it was difficult to have much of an effect, and even now it is still the case that the Lorenz story is not widely known.

A few months after Her Majesty's visit, a big breakthrough came from the award-winning film 'Codebreakers: Bletchley Park's Lost

Heroes', shown on BBC *Timewatch* and made by Julian Carey from BBC Wales. The programme focused on the Lorenz story – something I had been trying to achieve for a number of years. I was able to provide vital information for the programme and was glad to see the Testery, Bill Tutte and Tommy Flowers at last receive credit in it. The programme was televised for the first time on BBC2 on 25 October 2011. As far as I know, it has been shown four times on BBC2 and is estimated to have had more than 10 million viewers in the UK so far, as well as having appeared on history channels with audiences from many other countries. The film has been translated into different languages worldwide. A huge result, especially compared to the relatively tiny audiences present at most of my talks.

Through the campaign I came to know so many good people who gave me great encouragement and generous support. Some of them have become good friends. With public support and help, I have been able to achieve quite a lot during the campaign years. I managed to establish a better appreciation of the achievements of Tutte and the Testery. There were a number of initiatives which turned out to be successful, making a positive contribution to Bletchley Park while also improving awareness of the Lorenz story.

When I look back over the last six years, I am pleasantly surprised at how many initiatives of different kinds I have been able to undertake. Very gradually, things have happened and progress has been made, especially during the last couple of years. It has meant hard work but has been very worthwhile. My biggest contribution was in inspiring and helping Julian Carey to make the BBC *Timewatch* programme. Without Julian's help, the Lorenz story would have taken much longer to emerge. I was glad to see Tutte's profile raised and am very grateful to Julian.

During my campaign, my wife Mei has played an invaluable part, driving me anywhere and everywhere, remembering the things I have forgotten, dealing with emails and appointments, searching for contacts on the internet, typing and writing whenever I needed it. She has always been on hand, a real work partner and a loyal wife. She has been a supportive strength for me all the way and I cannot thank her enough. The new chairman at Bletchley Park, Sir John Scarlett, and Iain Standen, CEO, gave Mei a 'Lifetime Friend of Bletchley Park' award in July 2013. It was a wonderful surprise for her and we were both touched by that. A number of Bletchley Park Trustees and staff attended the award event for a formal presentation by Sir John. Indeed, Mei has always followed the fortunes of Bletchley Park with great interest and worked closely with me on so many different things. Whatever contribution she made, it was pleasing and reassuring to know the Bletchley Park Trust has recognised it.

HOW IT ALL STARTED

In the early summer of 2002, I received a letter completely out of the blue. It came from New Zealand, which seemed rather strange because I did not know anybody at all in New Zealand. It turned out to be a letter from Jack Copeland, a professor of philosophy at Canterbury University. He had obtained my details from Bletchley Park and he wrote to invite me to provide a chapter about the Testery for a book that he was putting together called *Colossus: The Secrets of Bletchley Park's Codebreaking Computers*. I gladly agreed, and within a week I had produced the text for my chapter.

After a couple of months he came across to Britain himself and we met in my flat in St George's Square, Westminster. Professor Copeland is a tall guy, about 6ft 3in plus, around 50 years of age, with a mop of curly fair hair, specs, and an easy-going and quietly spoken manner. He and I discussed the chapter and his work. He told me that Lorenz had been declassified. The secret had been kept for nearly sixty years after the war and it was now possible to talk and write about it. I was amazed and delighted. I had given no thought at all for all these years to my time during the war at Bletchley Park after I had left it in 1945. Apart from anything else, I had signed the Official Secrets Act in 1941 at Bletchley Park, which forbade me from ever speaking about anything connected with my work on Lorenz, and for nearly six decades after the war I was still bound by it.

During Jack's research for his forthcoming book, he had decided to work on two other books first. They related to Alan Turing (*The Essential Turing* (OUP USA, 2004) and *Alan Turing's Automatic Computing Engine* (OUP, 2005) and he had already started them, so he was keen to complete those first.

Eventually, in 2005, he contacted me again to continue working on *Colossus*. Jack got all the contributions together, wrote a number of chapters himself and the *Colossus* book finally appeared in the spring of 2006. The contributors to the book included a number of the top brains at Bletchley Park such as Tommy Flowers (Thomas H. Flowers), Bill Tutte (William Thomas Tutte), Max Newman, Jack Good, Donald Michie, Roy Jenkins, Helen Currie (née Pollard), Peter Edgerley, Peter Hilton, Gil Hayward, Harry Fensom, myself and many others. This book brought together contributions from key veterans who had worked at Bletchley Park or were associated with it, including members of the Testery and the Newmanry who worked on Lorenz. Other contributors were professionals like Tony Sale with his team, who built a replica of the wartime Colossus machine, a tremendous contribution to the exhibition at Bletchley Park.

Jack told me he was very glad to have found me. He said I was an important survivor as I knew all about the Testery from the beginning to the end, including the period when there were no machines, but also when the machines were used to help speed up some of the hand-breaking processes in the Testery. He was very keen to know more details about manual processing in the Testery, but also about the cryptographers' machines in the Newmanry. By this time in 2005 I was the last of the three original senior codebreakers on Lorenz, as Peter Ericsson and Denis Oswald had both died. The three of us had broken the majority of the Lorenz traffic right to the end of the war. When I thought about it, vivid memories came back immediately – old habits die hard. I was able to make my contribution, and it proved relatively easy to write my piece for Jack.

The *Colossus* book was, I think, a groundbreaking work. Jack laid out in great detail how Colossus had been used in the later stages of the breaking of Lorenz. It also showed for the first time how the top-level

Lorenz cipher system was broken initially by Bill Tutte and then the process of the daily message breaking by the Testery.

For the *Colossus* book, only three of the cryptographers from the Testery could contribute: Peter Hilton, Peter Edgerley and myself. In the book, we tended to cover the same ground so Jack had to cut things back to avoid repetition. For instance, the chapter that I provided was scaled back from eighteen to eleven pages. My original text had to cover the whole of my time at Bletchley Park, from 1941 to 1945. I also included a timetable of the events in the breaking of Lorenz, a list of personnel in the Testery and a map I made from my memory showing how the major Lorenz links gradually spread over Europe.

Somehow, Jack mentioned that I joined Bletchley Park in 1942 – he probably was not aware that I was actually one of the founder members of the Testery in 1941 and I had worked earlier on Double Playfair for a few months. (It was only after Tutte's breakthrough that the Testery was switched to breaking Lorenz traffic on 1 July 1942.) However, in the *General Report on Tunny* (see link at the end of this book to view a copy of the report) it stated that the Testery was established in July 1942. Again, this was not correct and quite misleading. I wanted to mention it here once more, just to set the record straight. But the 1945 *General Report on Tunny* was written by three people – Jack Good, Donald Michie and Geoffrey Timms – all from the Newmanry, after the war, and they did not invite any input from the people who had been in the Testery. In fact, the Newmanry machine team became active from mid 1943, so they were not really aware of the Testery's earlier work, including the first year and a half when we were breaking Lorenz entirely by hand.

Helen Currie (née Pollard), one of the first senior ATS typists in the Testery, also contributed a chapter for Jack and told her story. Helen and I had been put in touch with each other by Ian Munro, one of the Bletchley Park volunteers who had worked there for ten years and did such a great job helping Bletchley Park. He also introduced me to Edna Cooper, another wartime colleague at Bletchley Park. I was so pleased to be in touch with them, but we were all in our late 80s. Ian had come to know them both when they made visits to the Park. Ian and his wife, Rose, became good friends of ours; they left this country two years ago to join their only child, Mark, in Vancouver, Canada. We still keep in touch over Skype or by phone.

Jack's book was also the catalyst for me getting back in touch with Peter Hilton and Peter Edgerley. For a few years, we met once a year in London. Sadly, they have both died now. Both Peters joined the Testery towards the end of 1942. Peter Hilton had previously been working on Enigma, while Peter Edgerley was a new recruit. The three of us were able to contact each other and compare notes; this gave us a chance to exchange old memories for the first time ever. I was very pleased to be able to discuss the work we had done at Bletchley Park and this was very valuable in recording their impressions and details about what they had done. These slender links were much appreciated by the three of us.

Peter Edgerley told me he had kept quite a number of working papers instead of surrendering them to be destroyed on the orders of Churchill, so he was able to include more detail in his chapter. In a way it was good, as such material is valuable now, but he could have been in big trouble for this at the time and taken to court. I was a good boy and gave all mine up. I never thought to keep anything, except for the list of personnel in the Testery. This has been invaluable too, for helping quite a number of family and friends seeking their loved ones.

I met Peter Edgerley with his wife when they came to London once a year with their local group from Welwyn Garden City – located north of London. Each time, we would meet at the Royal Festival Hall on South Bank, just across the river from where I lived in St George's Square, Pimlico. We would have lunch together and talk about our days at Bletchley Park.

Peter Hilton, who had emigrated to the US in the 1960s, came over almost every year with his wife Maggie, but only for a week per year. They were both British, so would come over to see their family. We met them in 2003 and then for the next few years. I was very sad to discover that Peter had become seriously ill with dementia, and he died within a year. I wrote an obituary for him in the *Daily Mail* in 2010.

Before the publication of the book *Colossus* in 2006, I had also been in touch with people like Tom Colvill and Ralph Tester, who were former colleagues at the Testery. We were pleased with the reconnection. I was also to see Roy Jenkins, and we had drinks either at my flat or else at the House of Lords from around 2000 onwards, although we did not talk about Lorenz at all as it was still classified. Roy died soon afterwards following heart surgery in 2003, without knowing anything about the campaign to expose the Lorenz story. I realised that Roy had an outstanding mind, which he demonstrated as a historian and writer, as well as in his function as a politician. He made a huge impact in each of these spheres. He had not been a good codebreaker at Bletchley Park, but he was one of the very few with an immense intellect and was very friendly and down to earth.

JACK AND I

Professor Jack Copeland and I have been good friends for more than ten years now, since he contacted me in relation to his *Colossus* in 2002. We worked well together on a number of occasions. Whereas my primary interest is in seeking greater recognition for Bill Tutte and the Testery, Jack's main interest is in Alan Turing, a subject on which he is an expert. He has written a number of books about Turing. I contributed a chapter in Jack's latest work, *The Turing Guide*, at his request. Jack has done a great job bringing Turing's work to the attention of the British public and he also raised awareness of Tommy Flowers and the use of the Colossus computer, the technology that so radically changed the world we live and work in today.

In 2007, I was asked by Jack to give a talk about my wartime experiences on Lorenz. I was delighted to do this and it was the first time that I had visited Bletchley Park since I left in 1945. On a very dark November night, in the Ballroom, to a full house, I shared a session with Jack. We each gave a talk for around forty minutes. It proved to be really very interesting. This laid the foundations and gave me confidence to undertake further activities, all begun at the age of 87.

At the time, Bletchley Park was going through a difficult phase. Their financial position was extremely tight and most people worked there as volunteers. I hope my talks could be useful to increase Bletchley Park's profile and potentially to raise money.

Today, the picture at Bletchley Park is a very different one, with more activities, new exhibits and more interest. Millions more people are aware of the Lorenz story, mostly from the film 'Codebreakers: Bletchley Park's Lost Heroes', but also from other sources. It is good to know that Lorenz has been taken into account at Bletchley Park now. I credit this also to the new leadership at Bletchley Park in recent years. Under Sir John Scarlett, Iain Standen and their new team (including the new media manager Katharine Lynch) are helping to spread the word about the Lorenz story in different ways.

Over the years, I have always appreciated that Jack involved me in his book on Colossus and the talk at Bletchley Park. I introduced him and his book to many other people at my numerous talks and in my articles, and whenever Jack visited the UK I would try to provide something of interest to him.

In November 2008, through one of my contacts, there was a possibility of a film being made about the Lorenz story by Diverse, a TV production company in London introduced to me by Rory Cellan-Jones, the BBC's technology correspondent. I arranged for Jack to join me at the meeting and it was initially a success. The producers even asked us to write a synopsis, which I provided. After a month or so, there was no money available for such a programme and that was the end of the story. Another time, I invited Jack to visit the BBC TV Centre in White City for an interview with Rory Cellan-Jones, and sometimes we visited Bletchley Park together.

Another golden opportunity arrived in the summer of 2011 when Julian Carey, the BBC Wales producer, came to me about making a film. I introduced Jack and his *Colossus* book to the BBC *Timewatch* programme. The resulting documentary film is all about the Lorenz story and how two men – Bill Tutte and Tommy Flowers – changed the world and then disappeared from history. I was pleased that both great men got full credit for their achievements working on Lorenz.

Somehow, so he told me a number of times, Jack never watched the film, because he felt he would probably think there was too much about Tutte in it. In fact, this programme was awarded two BAFTAs in 2012 for the best documentary, and an international award in 2013. Julian Carey certainly deserves his medals for that!

Last year, I had a wonderful 92nd birthday. Jack kindly gave me a copy of his latest book, *Turing* – it was the first book, hot off the press – with a nice message in it, 'Happy Birthday Jerry. Thanks for everything and all the best. Jack.' It was unexpected and a real treat. This was his third book about Turing.

For my birthday, which fell on a Sunday, I had been invited by the CEO of Bletchley Park to pay a visit. There were two important groups visiting the Park, one from Google and the other from Silicon Valley in the US – more than 100 people in total. When we arrived at Bletchley Park, they wanted me to give a short talk, which I was glad to do as always. We all gathered in the lovely Ballroom in the Mansion House and received a very special introduction by Sir John Scarlett (the chairman) and Mr Iain Standen (CEO). We all had a lovely buffet lunch with soft drinks.

Quite suddenly, they surprised me by presenting a huge birthday cake and asking if I would blow out the candles. It was a wonderful surprise and I was very touched. It was a really heart-warming and splendid occasion. For this particular visit, Bletchley Park had colluded with my wife without me knowing about it. I gave a short speech and shared the cake with everybody. I did not even know that Jack was coming that day and I was very pleased to see him again. That is why, whenever Bletchley Park asked me to go for an event I was always delighted to accept without question. I felt valued by Bletchley Park – it was like a homecoming each time I visited.

About two years ago, Jack offered to help me write a book about the Lorenz story and I was pleased and agreed. Tutte is the third and less well-known of the three unsung heroes at Bletchley Park, but he was even more important in my view and so I expected a book about Tutte and Lorenz. I was keen to co-operate with Jack. I started to put the contents together for a number of chapters, to be divided between us. Jack would be the best as he is such a good writer and already well known in this field, and he thought I would make a good partner due to my knowledge about the subject and I had actually been there, did the work myself and knew the tricks, particularly to get that first vital break-in.

I waited and waited, but nothing came of the book. I realised that Jack was very busy with the amount of Turing related work on his hands and I decided quickly that I should write my own autobiography instead. Two years later, Jack mentioned again that we should collaborate to produce a book on Lorenz. However, by then I was 92 and had already spent two months on my own autobiography about my work at Bletchley Park. I was very eager to push ahead with that project, which many friends had been encouraging me to write.

HOW BLETCHLEY PARK WAS SAVED

After the war, at Bletchley Park the GC&CS changed its name officially to GCHQ (the Government Communications Headquarters) and then later moved to Cheltenham. However, the Code & Cipher School for training continued at the Park for the next forty years or so.

Bletchley Park is in a blessed location: it is well connected in all directions, with convenient access to Bletchley railway station and close proximity to several major roads. But, as it is set in 55 acres of land, it was nearly sold to housing developers in the 1990s, when planning permission was granted to demolish Bletchley Park and build hundreds of new houses on the site. Luckily, there was a small group of local people who started a campaign to save the Park for the nation. They set up the Bletchley Park Trust and developed it into a major heritage site to preserve the history of how and why the computer was invented and tell the story of how the site was home to so many Second World War codebreakers and the inspirational work they did there. I am so pleased to see it is now a wonderful museum open to the public and known worldwide.

Bletchley Park is the spiritual home of cryptology. It is also the birthplace of the computer and a historic site of immense importance for codebreaking and the war in general. There was a great opportunity to enlarge its image by promoting the great success of Enigma and, of course, the Lorenz story there. When I began my efforts and visited Bletchley Park in 2007, I could see the value of developing the site as a heritage centre as quickly as possible. I was concerned about the absence of the Lorenz story at the time, although I could see that the Trust needed the money first and so I understood their concentration on Enigma at the time. In my earlier talks I would always try to raise the subject of funds.

I remember after my talk at Google in 2009, the very next day they immediately raised substantial funds for Bletchley Park. Over the years they have always been supporters of Bletchley Park and are, in a number of ways, a great organisation. When I compare the situation six years ago, there has been an amazing improvement following the constant pressure and steady help from many people, volunteers and veterans like myself.

Tony Sale (1931–2011)

Tony was one of the people responsible for saving Bletchley Park in the early 1990s and a key person in understanding its unique value as a historic site and the home of the cryptographers during the Second World War. Tony is probably best known for leading the team that rebuilt the Colossus machine to exhibit in the Bletchley Park Museum. He was a fine engineer and had great ambition.

Rebuilding Colossus was a huge task. It had to be exactly the same machine as Tommy Flowers' wartime Colossus, which had been destroyed after the war. There was no money and the project had to be run on a purely voluntary basis, but Tony led his team and went ahead anyway. With his persistence and determination, it took him thirteen years to complete the work. His amazing contribution of the replica Colossus now stands impressively in Block H at the National Museum of Computing, which attracts so many visitors, not only to bring in income, but also adding to the Park's reputation. I feel we owe Tony a large debt of gratitude in helping to retain Bletchley Park as a museum today.

Volunteers' Help

Bletchley Park Trust was set up in 1992, started by a group of good people, all volunteers. I wonder whether this kind of maniacal devotion is purely a British phenomenon or whether it happens in other countries as well? I also wonder, if Tony Sale had not succeeded in rebuilding Colossus, what would Bletchley Park look like today? Probably a fine collection of suburban houses with the historic huts all knocked down. Simon Greenish was the new director at that time and recognised Tony's contribution. Simon's work in developing Bletchley Park made a huge difference – it should never be underestimated.

In the meantime, the trust had no money to play with. Most of the people who worked there were local volunteers, but some of the volunteers did not live locally and they had to pay their own travel costs to get to Bletchley Park. Many of them have a great passion to support Bletchley and since 2007 I have visited the Park very often. I came to know many good people like Kelsey Griffin, Simon Greenish, Sue May, Tony Sale and his wife Margaret, Frank Carter, John Gallehawk, John Chapman, Ian Munro, Philip Hays, Phil Le Grand, and later Katharine Lynch, Sir John Scarlett, Iain Standen and many more. Many have become good friends.

One of these friends, Ian Munro, volunteered at Bletchley Park regularly every Saturday, in spite of the fact that he had to travel from Littlehampton on the south coast to Bletchley and back – a return journey of four hours on the train. Fortunately, he had worked on the railways and so at least had his travel free in his retirement, but was giving up his four hours every week just to travel. Added to the eight hours that he worked there, it meant that he, in effect, had a twelve-hour working day. He was passionately interested in the Park and he put up with it for ten years until he emigrated to Vancouver, Canada, with his wife to join their son there.

As a Bletchley Park veteran myself, I have heard a number of stories of so many people voluntarily giving up their spare time and it has really moved me. Bletchley Park has become a warm and welcoming place now, with a lot of activities going on and a fascinating place for the visitors. Each time I visit, there is so much to see and always something new.

Over time, Bletchley Park has improved its financial position substantially and offers visitors a variety of exhibits, such as working Enigma machines, the Bombe rebuild, interactive displays and so on. As a result, this kind of self-help combines to make the Park interesting for the visitor and generates more income. The volunteers and staff have worked so hard and been rewarded by seeing the visitor numbers increase significantly over the last six years. This has been a huge success in securing Bletchley Park's future.

Bletchley Park now has the resources to present its fascinating story well and to make use of the museum to reach out to the public. They also received substantial funding from a variety of organisations such as English Heritage, the Lottery Fund, Google and several others. There was £480,000 support from the government through the Foreign Office, as well, announced by William Hague during a visit the Park in October 2012. Bletchley Park now is fully secured for the future.

CONTACTING THE MEDIA

Once the Lorenz story had been declassified, it was important to get the story across to the public as soon as possible. It needed new material and I made a number of efforts to bring the Lorenz story to the attention of the general public. Since 2007, with Mei's help, I began to use the internet to contact people, especially in the media, the national press or anywhere we could think of to help in spreading the word about Lorenz. We wrote a one-page story for the media informing them about Lorenz and inviting them to contact me. There was very little response at that time because people had never heard of Tutte and Lorenz and did not seem interested.

I started to notice particular interest in the *Daily Telegraph*, which I bought every day. I made contact with Charles Moore first. I did not know him personally, but I saw his articles almost every Saturday. He was a regular contributor and had a senior editorial position. I wrote him a personal letter and delivered it myself to its offices in Buckingham Palace Road, which is not far from where I lived. About ten days later, I received a response from Moore explaining that he was no longer on the staff at the paper but had gone freelance. However, he later passed on my letter to the relevant editor, but unfortunately the editor told him that the *Telegraph* had done quite a lot on the Enigma story fifteen years ago and now had no interest in Bletchley Park subjects. It was disappointing news, but Charles continued to try to help by introducing me to his friends who worked for *The Spectator*. I got in touch with them, but received no answer. The *Daily Telegraph* missed a great opportunity to get on board with the Lorenz story and I never contacted them again. We have failed in our efforts to reach out to other newspapers too.

BBC History Magazine

By now it was 2008 and the first successful contact we made via the internet had come through. This was from Robert Attar, the editor of *BBC History* magazine. He rang me and then sent me an email listing about twenty questions that he wanted to put to me over the course of a phone interview on the following day. I was very happy to follow this up. Soon after, his article appeared in the July 2008 edition of the magazine headlined 'Codebreaker Jerry Roberts' claim for proper recognition of Bletchley Park Heroes', which was placed in the 'Breaking News' section with a full-page story.

Robert also put my phone interview on a podcast and advertised it in the magazine, so people could hear our conversation about the Lorenz story. This conversation with Robert, about twenty minutes on the podcast, took place on Wednesday 18 June 2008 and can still be downloaded from the BBC magazine website (see link at the end of this book).

This was a great encouragement after nearly a year of activity. I was very grateful for Robert's help – a young editor who had good vision. Robert later sent me a generous personal letter, saying how grateful he was on behalf of Britain for the work my colleagues and I had done.

He said that without the vital work of the codebreakers at Bletchley Park, the war would have carried on longer and his family, who were Jews, would not have survived. I was very pleased and much moved by his story.

Rory Cellan-Jones' Help

In the summer of 2008, I saw a banner headline, 'Saving Bletchley Park', in the *Telegraph*, contributed by Dr Sue Black. The article led to a petition signed by 200 scientists and computer experts in favour of saving Bletchley Park. I rang her and told her about my interest in the Park and she came to visit us in our home at Pimlico, with her youngest daughter, Leah, who was aged 6. We chatted for about two hours and established a lot of common ground. She was very excited to meet me and hear the Lorenz cipher story, of which she had not been aware, especially coming direct from a real Lorenz codebreaker.

Dr Black established a blog called 'Saving Bletchley Park' (see end of this book for the link). To this she added the news of our chat on her website diary the very next day. Sue had developed many contacts through her Bletchley Park campaign. She kindly introduced me to Rory Cellan-Jones, one of the senior correspondents in technology at the BBC. Soon Rory and his colleague, Mark Ward (a BBC web designer), came along to see me – twice in a week at our home. I was very excited, as the BBC seemed to be really keen! We talked for about two hours. I gave them the whole story and allowed them to use it for whatever purpose they wanted. Rory realised it was an important story and said he would like to help in any way he could. He found it extremely interesting and appeared very positive, and he was keen to do something about it, possibly making a TV programme.

In October 2008, Rory sent a cameraman, Andrew Webb, to carry out an interview and to film me over a six-hour day at my London home; he left at 8 p.m. that night. We were very excited and hoped it would be used for making a BBC programme on Lorenz.

I rang Rory from time to time, but nothing appeared to happen. Later, Rory told me that no programme was possible because the BBC did not have any money to spare. However, the BBC would keep the story in their archive and he would like to keep in touch with me. After a couple of years, Andrew did manage to put two short clips (about five minutes each) onto the BBC website.

In early November 2008, Professor Jack Copeland came to the UK from New Zealand. I always liked to meet Jack and had arranged something interesting for him during his visit. I got in touch with Rory again, and this time we were invited to his office at the BBC Television Centre, White City. Jack and I had another interview with Rory and Mark, very friendly and efficiently as usual. They put our interview on the BBC website the next day, entitled 'Code-cracking and computers'.

A few months later in early 2009, I was interviewed again, this time by another division, the BBC History Channel, represented by Michelle Milner. She came with her professional cameraman and spent another few hours at our home interviewing and filming me.

I waited and waited, and still – absolutely nothing. That too went into the icebox. It was another disappointment. I asked myself, why is there no money to make such an important programme? Is the BBC really not interested? Wouldn't they find the money wherever they could? I was very worried this piece of history might not get to be recorded, because by then there were only three of us codebreakers left who had worked directly on Lorenz and we were in our late 80s. Peter Hilton lived in the US and Peter Edgerley was quite ill by then, so I could not expect help from them, but I felt I had a duty to do something about it and I couldn't afford to wait.

The BBC never offered to pay me anything for those two long interviews, all they did was ask me to sign an agreement so that they could use my interview for any purpose. I did not mind this; I gave many talks, articles and interviews and have never asked for payment. My concern was to get the story out as soon as possible, as I was not getting any younger and time was marching onwards. I did wonder, though, if maybe because the BBC had got my information for free, they held no value in it. I was disappointed that nothing had happened for the following three and a half years. It shows how hard it was in the early days to get people interested in the story.

Rory Cellan-Jones was still keen and willing to help in any way he could, but the answer from the BBC was always that there was no money available to make a programme. I kept in regular touch with him, but he couldn't do any more as this was not in his area of control.

CONTACTING FILM-MAKERS

Rory Cellan-Jones was always positive, friendly and supportive. He suggested to me that I should get in touch with one of the production companies which made films for the BBC. Rory explained that the BBC mostly bought programmes from them. This idea led me to contact a number of companies who were all interested. One of them, called Diverse TV, in Kensington, near Hammersmith in London, was particularly enthusiastic. They arranged a meeting within a few days. I contacted Jack while he was still in this country and he was very excited about the prospect. I took him along with me to the meeting on 12 November 2008.

At Diverse, the producer, Mark Roberts, the executive producer, Ed Crick and two of their colleagues all came to the meeting with Jack and myself. We had a great opportunity to discuss with them the possibilities of making a film for a TV programme. They told us that they had nearly 100 wartime stories, but Lorenz was by far the most interesting. We discussed the whole project, we even agreed the terms and the percentages between all three parties, including the BBC, and they asked me to write a synopsis for a possible programme.

I wrote the synopsis in a couple of weeks and they were happy with it. It sounded extremely promising; everything looked rosy. Jack rang me from New Zealand from time to time to check on progress; we were both very excited. A few weeks later, I had a call from Diverse in which they said that they couldn't go ahead, because the main contact at the BBC had left the company and Diverse themselves had no money to fund a film. Jack and I were greatly disappointed.

In spring 2009, we contacted another private film-making company called Find a TV Expert. We spoke with Claire Richmond, who had successfully made a number of well-known series for the BBC and had worked there for more than ten years. She started her own film production company. After a few phone conversations, Claire was clearly interested in my story and was considering involving her friend, John Bullivan, from another company, to work on the production together. However, John was too busy and maybe wasn't so keen and he missed two appointments. So Claire sent another contact to meet me at my home.

This time it was Sinclair McKay. He turned out to be a writer, not a film-maker, which was not what I was looking for. He told me he had previously worked with the *Daily Telegraph*, was now a freelancer and he knew Charles Moore (with whom I had been in touch earlier). Sinclair and I chatted and I gave him a two-hour interview over lunch.

I forgot about the meeting after that, but a year later, in July 2010, I received a copy of his book, *The Secret Life of Bletchley Park* (Aurum Press, 2010), since I was one of the people who had contributed by telling their stories. That was a nice surprise: it all helped spread the word about Tutte and Lorenz. Two years later, I received a copy of a file from Bletchley Park. It was Sinclair's recording of the whole conversation and was another unexpected pleasure.

20

A SELECTION OF MY TALKS

MY FIRST TWO TALKS AT UCL

I have given many one-hour talks about my wartime work during the last six years. Here, I have selected a few about which I have particular memories.

Normally, I prepared a single page of notes as a guide for my talks, with about twenty visuals to illustrate key points. I was very conscious of my responsibility to draw the attention of the public to the whole story of Lorenz and, in particular, to Bill Tutte's achievement in breaking the system and to the Testery's work. I still felt strongly the need to try to find more ways to make more contacts. Almost by accident, we found that talks proved very effective in achieving this objective. Through them, we came to know many good people and visited so many places. It has been very enjoyable. I managed to give many talks, but I never had any qualms at these events because I was fully in command of my material and knew that people would find it interesting. It was all for a very good cause.

My first talk was given at UCL, where I had taken my degree in German and French from 1939 to 1941. The talk was organised by my wife Mei and our daughter Chao. They put their heads together because they wanted to give me a surprise present for my birthday in November. Chao at the time was studying German at UCL, the same as I had all those years ago. She agreed to talk with her tutor, Stephanie Bird, and mentioned the possibility to the head of her

German department, Professor Susanne Kord, to see whether it would be possible to set up the talk in which I could recount the Lorenz story.

The answer came very soon: Professor Kord was very keen on the idea. She arranged to meet me. When she discovered that this was the first time I had set foot in the college, as the German department had been evacuated to Aberystwyth during the war, she kindly took me around the premises before we had lunch in the staff canteen. It was ironic that Professor Kord, who organised my talk about what I had done during the war against the Germans, was herself a German!

My first hour-long talk was given to an audience of around sixty or seventy German students and a few members of the general public. Dr Sue Black was there and had brought someone along from the BBC. The talk went very well, flowed well and there was great applause at the end. We all felt that we were working in the right direction. The talk was on my 88th birthday in November 2008.

Professor Kord was very interested and she felt greatly encouraged by the enthusiastic response from students who sent her emails and wanted to know more about the subject. She thought it was important to get my story across to the public. She set up a second talk for me, on a much bigger scale. The date was set for the New Year 2009, by which time staff and students would have returned to their work. This time she booked UCL's theatre, which could accommodate up to 500 people, although it wasn't available until March.

She advertised the event on their website and the result was amazing:

Captain Jerry Roberts, UCL German alumnus and Second World War codebreaker, talk at UCL on 11 March 2009. The last British survivor of the cryptographers who worked on Tunny in the Testery at Bletchley Park.

I was delighted and set about preparing for the talk which covered the subject pretty well in a way that could be interesting to the general public. It was all very tentative at that stage. We were feeling our way and none of us had any experience in operating such events. However, that evening everything went really well and at the end, the audience kept applauding for a long time. It gave me a warm feeling and great satisfaction. It was a full house and there were a further 570 people on the waiting list. Guests comprised UCL alumni, staff, students and members of the public, including members of the 'Save Bletchley Park' campaign. The talk was fully booked within days. All tickets were free of charge.

This also gave me much encouragement for future talks. I realised that there was a phenomenal interest in the whole subject and we were all very pleased. At first Susanne considered repeating the event for the people on the waiting list, but then she decided to put my talk on the internet and on iTunes so everybody could watch it. Ever since, my UCL talk has been available online (see link at the end of this book).

For this talk, I was introduced by the provost, Sir Malcolm Grant, first, then Susanne gave an excellent introduction with a real touch of humour. She must have been very pleased with how the evening had developed, as indeed I was. I was greatly relieved that things had passed off well, as I was not used to public speaking on a big stage to audiences of that size. After the talk, it was clear that Sir Malcolm was also very pleased with the way the whole evening had gone. He had arranged drinks for everybody and set up a private dinner for twelve of us, including himself, his wife, the three of us in my family and of course Susanne with her husband John. Another of the guests was Lord Geoffrey Dear, who was a good friend of the provost and also an alumnus of UCL.

Lord Geoffrey Dear, tall and distinguished-looking, had been a law student at UCL in the 1960s. Ever since the event, we have been friends. He promised me if any opportunities occurred, he would like to help with the cause. He was as good as his word. Indeed, he later tried to promote a motion in the House of Lords to give Tutte a suitable award. However, the motion was declined unfortunately, because other members of the House felt this was all a long time ago, it should have been sorted out at the end of the war and it was not relevant now.

However, I hold a very different view. There had been a long delay in revealing the story because of the Official Secrets Act – the story had been kept secret for more than sixty years before it was revealed to the public. How can such heroes at Bletchley Park ever get the recognition they deserve? The government, which had done absolutely nothing about Tutte's achievement, has still done absolutely nothing. This is typical of the great divide between the cryptographers and members of the armed forces, who get generous and early recognition in the form of promotion or honours. The codebreakers who gave important service to their country received nothing. This was true for Turing, Tutte and for Dilly Knox as well. It was also the case for Tommy Flowers. In my view, they could be given a statue somewhere in central London, even Trafalgar Square or Parliament Square, it would not be too much considering the impact they had on modern life.

The two talks had given me great confidence and I realised that I could spread the word very effectively through other talks. At that stage, I still had no special contacts, no people in high places – except within UCL which had given my story a big boost.

A TALK AT ST JAMES'S PLACE INTERNATIONAL

On 27 February 2009, I gave a talk to a very different group of people. This time it was organised by one of my financial advisors, Robert MacDonald, a senior partner of St James's Place International (SJP) for their financial group. I was first put in touch with them in 1994 by Patrick Cogan, a friend of mine who worked there. SJP operated then under the Rothschild name.

Robert is a dynamic person and he arranged seminars regularly for his investors. They used their seminars to publicise their investment bonds, of which they want to sell more to the general public. The purpose was to promote their services to potentially new and existing clients.

He invited me to give a talk about my Bletchley Park experience to their staff and leading clients at one of his seminars. I was pleased to do this as it opened up a completely new area for spreading the word. In addition, he organised and published an article which featured my story in their glossy magazine, *The Investor*, in the winter issue 2010. It covered three pages and had a colour photo of the Lorenz machine on the front cover.

Again the talk appeared to arouse a lot of interest. It was an extremely positive atmosphere and there were many friendly questions during the buffet lunch provided by Robert. More than 100 people attended. They held the talk in a very attractive, large, handsome historic house – Avington Park, near the town of Winchester. The house was transformed in the late seventeenth century for Charles II to stay.

MY TALK AT GOOGLE

One day, in the middle of August 2009, I had a phone call out of the blue. This was from Mark Detre, who invited me to go to Google and give a talk to their staff. Mark had heard my talk at UCL a few months earlier and was impressed. He was another alumnus of UCL and he had also studied in the German department. He was then a senior executive at Google HQ in Buckingham Palace Road, central London. The talk date was set for 24 August.

After having lunch, we went to a room where more than 100 people were already seated – a full house in the largest room at Google. Many of them were seated on the floor to listen as all the seats were full. The staff there were all in their late 20s or their 30s.

The people attending were curious and understood well the contribution made by Bletchley Park during the war. After my talk finished, one of the Google staff gave out donation details for anyone interested in helping the Park. This was very effective. The donations immediately rolled in and proved to be of considerable benefit to Bletchley Park.

Next day, Mark Detre sent me a wonderful email:

Dear Jerry,

Thank you ever so much for coming in to speak yesterday. We have already received many warm comments about your talk; many people came up to me afterwards to say how compelling they found it and there is discussion around the whole company this morning of individuals' donations to Bletchley Park. I think Google staff were particularly captivated by the fact that you, when you went up to Bletchley Park, were younger than they are now (and we have a fairly young workforce here in general!) I'm sure that there will be many people going up to visit on the back of this talk.

All the best, Mark.

I was grateful to Mark for giving me the chance to talk there and pleased to see how efficient the Google people made it. He organised everything brilliantly and thoughtfully, and we all had a wonderful day. We came away with a fine impression of Google as an organisation. I was very impressed by Google staff making donations to Bletchley Park so soon after my talk. It was also nice to know that the talk went on YouTube afterwards.

Ever since, there has been a link between Google and Bletchley Park. They gave the Park a great deal of support, such as at the Enigma Reunion, an annual event held at Bletchley Park, where they provided the food and drink for the veterans. A month after my talk, the veterans had their reunion at Bletchley Park as usual and there were large numbers of people present, including a number from television and press. The guests enjoyed a first-class buffet lunch which had all been supplied by Google and its staff.

However, it went a lot further than I expected. Bletchley Park at that time needed every penny they could lay their hands on. After this event, I have since learned from Dr Sue Black that her efforts in supporting the link with Bletchley Park and Google helped to bring in money and engender stronger public interest. She is amazing and helped Bletchley Park in many ways.

A TALK AT THE CHELTENHAM FESTIVAL, 2009

The Cheltenham Festivals are annual events covering science, music and literature and together are one of the UK's most important cultural institutions.

In October 2009 I was provided with another valuable opportunity to spread the word – this time, an excellent one. I would be able to reach a much larger audience (around 1,200 people). I was asked by Kelsey

Griffin from Bletchley Park to go up to the Cheltenham Literature Festival and take part in a Q&A session. We were very well treated by the organisers. We were picked up from our house in Liphook and driven all the way to Cheltenham and returned home the following day.

After arriving in Cheltenham Mei and I were picked up by Mr Tony Comer, the historian at GCHQ, who took us to visit the GCHQ building. We had requested to meet with the director, Iain Lobban, beforehand. He was already engaged that day, so Tony took us into their famous doughnut-shaped building instead. Security was very tight. We had to go through gate after gate.

Tony looked after us for the whole of that visit. We talked for nearly an hour about my work at Bletchley on Lorenz. He was very interested and it seemed that he had not known much about Lorenz before my visit. Tony introduced me to his colleague, the curator of their museum. She showed us around the main museum and I was amazed to spot an item which referred to my former tutor, Professor Leonard Willoughby, at UCL. It dated from his time at GCHQ during the First World War, when he had been a cryptographer and linguist decrypting messages sent by Germany and its allies.

After lunch, we went to do our stuff at the festival. On the large stage at the festival, I was joined by Oliver Lawn, who was one of the top codebreakers on Enigma, and his wife, Sheila Lawn, who had also worked at Bletchley Park. The chairperson, Peter Guttridge, a well-known crime fiction novelist, asked us questions alternately. We gave answers, each speaking for around twenty minutes over the course of the session. The session went very well followed by enthusiastic applause.

It was obvious that the whole subject of codebreaking struck a chord with the British public: every single event I have taken part in has had a full audience and elicited substantial applause at the end. The talk at Cheltenham was an all-ticket performance with a considerable audience of around 1,200 in the theatre hall, with spectators paying £7 a head to attend, which raised substantial funds for the organisation.

This was first time we had a really large audience and it was an interesting experience. We had a lot of questions from the floor, which Oliver and I were glad to deal with. When we finished there was great sustained applause and I felt our long journey had been well worthwhile. Afterwards we withdrew to a room called the Writer's Room, in which contributors like ourselves were offered tea, coffee and cake. Suddenly, Judie and James Hodsdon appeared; they had been part of the audience. The couple have had a long and continuous working relationship with GCHQ. Mrs Hodsdon had held senior positions at and had a lot of contact with Bletchley Park – and indeed I remember her. On several occasions at Bletchley Park she was a spokesperson on behalf of GCHQ and made a number of announcements. She is still one of the Trustees of Bletchley Park. Later I knew her father Sir Arthur Bonsall who was also a Bletchley Park veteran, having worked for Air Section in Hut 4.

By now, we had made a number of GCHQ friends and kept in touch with them from time to time. A year later, in June 2011, Tony Comer kindly approached Professor David Stupples to contact me about writing a joint book about Lorenz, Bill Tutte and the Testery story. I was glad and looked forward to co-operating with him. We met and discussed the possibilities and listed contents. But again, the project never got off the ground.

A TALK AT LATYMER

In September 2011, another bolt from the blue came when I was invited by my old school, Latymer Upper School in London, to give a talk to the students. As usual, I happily agreed and was excited, especially as I was an alumnus of the school. I was contacted at first by Mr Nigel Orton, a Director of Alumni Relations at the school, who set everything up for the talk. Mr Orton must have found me from coverage in the press of Her Majesty the Queen and me, when she paid a visit to Bletchley Park a couple of months earlier that year. He had also obtained the photograph of me with the Queen and used it in the school magazine *OLNEWS*.

A few days after the invitation, I found myself up on the platform in the school surveying a large number of students and a number of teachers in the main hall of Latymer. I had spent six years studying there and the surroundings were very familiar and yet, seen from the platform, it also seemed completely unfamiliar. In my time, it was a high-grade boys' school. The boys very seldom went up on that platform, unless perhaps to receive a prize at the annual prize-giving, as I had a number of times. This talk was totally different. I had no sense of nervousness and I felt completely at home, even though I had not been into the school since I had left. What a thrill – I was honoured to be invited back to Latymer after seventy-three years.

At Latymer, the walls of the hall were coved with boards showing the names of the boys who either held top positions at the school or been outstanding students and these went back many years. After the talk, I was introduced by Mr Orton to the headmaster of the school Mr Peter Winter and, later, his charming wife Adwoa who entertained us over lunch in the teachers' dining room. It would be difficult to find someone less like the head in my time. When I first went to Latymer in 1934, the headmaster was the Rev. Edmond Dale, who was a portly and sombre-looking man in his 60s. But the school flourished under him and it is still prosperous today under the much younger and crisper Mr Winter.

The talk went very well, as usual; I was given a good reception. I was pleased, as this was a good opportunity to tell our younger generation about Lorenz. After I got back home a few days later, I received a large envelope with a bundle of letters from Latymer students. It was heart-warming to read each of their comments and the feelings they expressed, which were positive and so appreciative. I also received a nice letter from Mr Winter himself, thanking me for giving the talk. One of the student letters that caught my eye was from Isabel von Stauffenberg. I immediately recognized the name from decrypts – the man who bravely planted the bomb to assassinate Hitler in 1944, so I asked Mr Orton whether she was any relation. Amazingly, she turned out to be from that family: Colonel von Stauffenberg was her great-great-uncle!

Recently, I received a letter from new headmaster David W. Goodhew at Latymer, telling me that my name will be added to the 'Distinguished List' in 2013. It was another honour and a wonderful surprise. I was delighted and it lifted my spirits greatly at my age. I feel I owe a great debt to Latymer for giving me such a great start in life.

21

MEETING HER MAJESTY QUEEN ELIZABETH II

On 15 July 2011, Her Majesty Queen Elizabeth II and the Duke of Edinburgh paid a visit to Bletchley Park. It was the first time that she had actually visited, although the Duke of Kent had visited two years earlier on 16 July 2009, which event I had attended.

Two weeks before, I received a phone call suggesting that I should go to Bletchley Park on the day, but not saying why in any precise terms. They only told me that it would be to meet a VIP. Two or three days before the event, I received a letter, which was more specific. It enclosed a formal invitation card, telling me the date and the time and indicating that I was one of seven people who would be presented to Her Majesty. It also gave instructions of how to behave in her presence and some indication of how to be dressed (more formally than usual). I was thrilled and delighted, as I had never met the Queen before. I was to meet her in Block B at the lower exhibition floor, home of the Naval Section in wartime and now part of the museum.

On the day, we reached Bletchley quite early, before 9 a.m. I was told that I would have an interview with Nicholas Witchell, the BBC royal correspondent. The interview went well and it was shown on BBC News. I couldn't watch it, obviously, until I got back home later that evening.

After my interview, I waited with the other six people who were to be presented to the Queen. When Her Majesty arrived I was the last on the list – by then it was around 11.45 a.m. Waiting for her was a rather nervous time and in the meantime I stationed myself by an actual Lorenz machine with its twelve wheels. When she came, I was able to point to the machine and explain to her what we had had to do during the war and the importance of what we had done. She seemed extremely interested and asked me four or five questions about it, each time with a wonderful smile. She was really interested and delightful. I told her the story and she spent something like seven or eight minutes with me, instead of the usual quick smile and handshake.

Afterwards, I saw the Duke of Edinburgh, accompanied by Simon Greenish, CEO of the Bletchley Park Trust, who was looking after him for the day. I was prepared to give the story again to the Duke, but he moved by at speed and I had the impression he was already thinking about his lunch, rather than Lorenz.

After meeting Her Majesty, we all went back up to ground level, by which time it was midday. The next item on the agenda for the Queen was to unveil an 8ft memorial carrying the words 'We Also Served'. She made a brilliant speech before the unveiling. There were a lot of journalists and photographers, and many school children there waving flags and making a lovely welcoming noise. We saw Her Majesty arrive by helicopter and leave in a Rolls-Royce.

I was interviewed by various media people that day. I told Nicholas Witchell about the work that I had done on Lorenz during the war in some detail, and also about Tutte and the Testery. I explained about the use of Colossus and how the machine helped in the breaking of Lorenz traffic. For this reason, I was rather surprised when I watched him speaking on BBC News that evening. He got most things right, but he did not say a word about the breaking of Lorenz – it was not mentioned in the news at all, and his comments were all about Enigma.

Even more astonishing, he pointed to a Bombe machine and he called it the Colossus and said it was used on Enigma. In fact, the Bombe machine helped on Enigma and the Colossus machine helped on Lorenz. Colossus was used only for helping to break Lorenz, never for Enigma. I sent him an email message the very next morning, explaining and pointing out the difference between these two cipher machines.

We were glad to see Bletchley Park receiving the recognition it so deserves. Altogether, it was an absolutely wonderful day. I greatly enjoyed seeing the memorial being unveiled. The whole occasion was crowned for me by meeting the Queen and by her delightful smile, which was recorded in a cherished photograph. It was taken by Sir Arthur Edwards, the *Sun* and royal photographer. I shall always remember with great affection those few minutes that I spent talking with her and listening to her.

22

BBC *TIMEWATCH*

The genesis of the BBC *Timewatch* programme was one of those happy accidents. I was invited to give a short talk at Bletchley Park on the opening day of The National Museum of Computing (TNMOC) on 26 May 2011. It was set up as an independent museum in Block H and continues the story of computing from where the main Bletchley Park story ended. The exhibits include Colossus, the recently rebuilt British Tunny and many others from the history of computing.

I was invited to attend by Tony Sale, because of my link with Lorenz. Helen Currie, one of the ATS girls, also gave a brief talk about the work she had done in the Testery. I was very interested in this new enterprise as it might give us the possibility of getting greater exposure for Bill Tutte and for the Testery. However, when I looked around their new exhibit there was very little about either. I had, in fact, prepared material about the Lorenz story for them and they agreed to put it up among their exhibits because that part of the story was missing, but they only put up a small part of it on a big board in the area close to the British Tunny machine which Helen had worked on – still not really enough, but at least part of the Lorenz story was being told at TNMOC.

At the opening, the Lorenz story was introduced by Tony Sale, followed by Andy Clark, a director of TNMOC, who generously said, 'We are greatly indebted to Jerry for helping us understand the context of Colossus.' I was glad that I had contributed something useful for Tutte and Lorenz.

Dr Stephen Fleming had interviewed me at my home to cover the Lorenz story a number of times, and TNMOC had made good use of it, putting it on their website. Andy Clark also said, 'The work of the team, led by John Pether and John Whetter is fantastic and, we hope, a fitting tribute to the achievements of the wartime codebreakers.' Indeed, the team of engineers made a major contribution by reproducing a British Tunny machine to be exhibited there (the original machines had all been destroyed after the war). By coincidence, I was told that Andy and I shared the same birthday, and since then when our birthdays came around we sent greetings to each other.

There were a couple of errors in their presentation which appeared on the BBC website the next day. For example, they said that Bill Tutte had been an engineer who had built the first Lorenz machine. This was not true, he had broken the Lorenz system without ever seeing the German Lorenz machine. Secondly, they said in the interview to the BBC that the British machine broke the Lorenz messages. This was, of course, a mistake. It implied that the codebreakers no longer had anything to do; that all the cryptographers could have packed up their things and gone home. In fact, we cryptographers had to break each day's traffic by hand to establish the wheel patterns even during the Colossus period. We were still an essential element in the whole Lorenz breaking process.

I found these errors quite extraordinary, but I do not blame them, since so little was known about the processing of Lorenz messages. I suggested to Dr Fleming, who handles PR for TNMOC, that corrections should be made to the BBC website and he quickly made the changes.

My talk at TNMOC led to a very lucky opportunity. It was quite a big crowd of a few hundred people for the opening, so I stepped over the rope and stood next to the exhibits and talked to the crowd and gave them the background to what the machines had done and the roles they had played in the breaking of Lorenz. My intervention, completely off-the-cuff, had remarkable and very favourable consequences. Fortunately, there was one person among that crowd who would later be very important to the whole Lorenz story. This was Julian Carey, one of the BBC's film producers from BBC Wales. He was impressed by my impromptu talk. I was able to say enough to arouse his interest and he spotted immediately that there was scope for his next programme and it was he who realised that there was a great story to tell.

A few days later I received a phone call from Julian. He explained that he had heard my talk at the opening of TNMOC. He realised that I was a key person from whom to obtain facts about the Lorenz story because I had actually worked on it. He asked if he could meet me for a two-hour interview at my home. I was delighted, and three days later he turned up on my doorstep. He brought with him cameraman Simon French, sound-man Chris Syner and editor Dina Mufti.

I had previously told Julian that I could spare him only twenty minutes as I had been disappointed a couple of times by the BBC in London, when they had made so many hours of film and then had not used it. Julian spent three hours with us altogether and filmed for about two hours. In the end, it was clear that Julian was fascinated by the whole story and he was delighted with my material and assured me, 'I promise you, Jerry, that I will make this programme. I am interested in the story and I want you to be proud of me.' This suggested that he was serious about it – and he was as good as his word.

This was exactly the kind of action I had hoped for all along, and it was such a relief to see something actually happening. Julian Carey was a very intelligent and far-sighted young man with a very positive approach that I really got to like. After the first time we met, Julian and I became friends and contacted each other quite frequently. I gave him a lot of background information and I recommended that he should get in touch with Jack Copeland. Julian planned at first to go with the whole crew to interview him in New Zealand, but eventually decided to use a local company. They conducted an interview with Jack – he talked more about Flowers and I talked more about Lorenz and Tutte. Julian used both of these extensively. I urged Julian to feature Bill Tutte strongly in the film.

Indeed, Julian Carey did a really good job on the Lorenz programme. It all built up into an extremely interesting film, and some weeks later, when he had put together the first cut, Mei and I drove to Cardiff. We had volunteered to look at the existing version and make any suggestions for improvements or corrections. In the end, it was a good job that we did this because there were about fifteen modifications needed, so it was a very worthwhile trip! However, it was clear that Julian had listened carefully to what I had laid out. He got almost all of the details right.

The BBC *Timewatch* programme finally came out on 25 October 2011, entitled, 'Codebreakers: Bletchley Park's Lost Heroes'. A link to a preview of the programme can be found at the end of this book. It is a fascinating documentary and presents a significant missing piece of history which had never been told on TV before. The programme won two British Academy Cymru Awards in 2012 and an international award in January 2013.

I have a lot to thank Julian for. I admire him enormously for spotting this great subject and for his determination in making the programme. He richly deserves the awards he later received. I do really hope others will follow up this story; there is still plenty of meat on the bone. It was extraordinarily lucky that Julian was present on that day at TNMOC and even luckier that I had got to my feet and made my impromptu talk about the importance of Lorenz. The programme helped to keep my campaign for greater recognition of all those who worked at Bletchley going. Without Julian taking this opportunity and making the film, it is entirely possible that it would have taken years for it to happen – if ever! We now have not just a film, but one which won a best documentary award in Britain and internationally.

Julian must have been pleased with the film's outcome and he must also have appreciated the collaboration. When the work on the film was finished and before it was broadcast, he sent me a fine email:

> Finally – the last word goes to you, Jerry – as it should – with the comment that this was a triumph of mind over machine. Thank you, Jerry, you've been an immeasurable help and an inspiration throughout – I did promise you back in June I'd do my best for you – I hope you think that was the case at the end of it all. Take care and we'll be in touch.
> All the best, Julian.

I am personally very grateful to Julian Carey for making this historic programme.

After the programme was shown in October 2011, I received a lot of fantastic feedback from family, friends and many others, even from abroad. Many people I didn't know also wrote letters and emails to me, some of them without my full address, and it was really heart-warming to read them. One of these letters was from my old school, Latymer, from the headmaster, Peter Winter. He wrote:

Codebreakers was broadcast. It is fascinating and extremely well made. What an interesting and poignant story! It is so good that it is now being told, albeit after so many years. Many congratulations to you for your part in the programme. I am very proud of the fact that a Latymerian (and a fellow linguist at that!) made such a distinguished contribution to defeating a tyranny. Best wishes, Peter.

I was also pleased that Rory Cellan-Jones commented on Twitter:

Capt Jerry Roberts wrote to me 3 years ago asking how to get a documentary made about Tunny at Bletchley. I wasn't any help … but he did it!

He sent a number of positive messages after this. Obviously, he was very pleased about the film coming out at last.

Mavis Batey, a senior Enigma codebreaker at Bletchley during the war, rang me and emailed me with her congratulations, saying, 'your Lorenz story at last appears, accurately told, I am so pleased for you'. She also told me at that time that Julian might help her make a film about Dilly Knox.

One of the other letters came from a friend, Lord Geoffrey Dear:

It was a very affirmative commentary on a splendid and noteworthy episode in our history and one that needs constant repetition to ensure that the present generation do not lose sight of all that was done by people such as you, for the benefit of those coming later. You must be very proud. I certainly am, for you! Warmest good wishes to you both, Geoff.

SCIENCE BRITANNICA

Recently there was another BBC TV series called *Science Britannica*, in which Tutte's story also featured in the second of the three episodes, called 'Method and Madness'. It was presented by Professor Brian Cox, who is a well-known presenter of science programmes for the BBC.

On 29 August 2012 I had to be at Bletchley Park for an appointment with BBC film director Rebecca Edwards and her team of six people, including Professor Cox. They came to visit the Park for the filming of *Science Britannica*.

Professor Cox had been searching for subjects for the programme and he immediately understood the significance of Tutte's achievement. He expressed it so well in the programme. He asked me a number of very intelligent questions, and our conversation was friendly and casual but of a good quality and I didn't feel nervous, perhaps because I have seen him already on TV a number of times. He always has that kind of knowledgeable, natural and friendly personality. Our conversation contributed a good eight minutes to the programme.

Professor Cox also explained how Tutte applied scientific methods to deduce the logical structure of the Lorenz machine. He said in the programme, 'Tutte broke the Tunny system by using logic, careful observation and by producing testable hypotheses, he managed to determine exactly how it worked.' The programme also showed in detail how Tutte's breaking of Lorenz influenced the course of the war. I thought it was well observed and did the story justice. I enjoyed seeing Tutte getting well-deserved coverage at last.

After the programme appeared on TV, I heard that Professor Cox received many questions from the public. The emails and tweets asked him why he mentioned Tutte rather than Turing, because most people had never heard of Tutte. Professor Cox's reply was short and crisp, 'Enigma is well known for breaking the naval code. Tutte is not well known for breaking Hitler's High Command code. You can compare it yourself.'

Professor Cox did a great job in raising the profile of Tutte. If there is more help from the media, I am sure one day Tutte will get the same amount of recognition as Turing.

23

THE TURING CENTENARY LECTURE

The year 2012 was Alan Turing's 100th birthday anniversary. Two special celebratory events were organised by Professor Jack Copeland, a leading authority on Turing, and Huma Shah, a leading scientist at the University of Reading. They had both been preparing these events for nearly a year.

TALKS AT KING'S COLLEGE

Our first talk took place at King's College Cambridge on 15–16 June. Turing had studied there. The conference lasted for three days and there were about eighteen talks given by people from relevant professions, computer experts and so on. Brian Oakley CBE, a Trustee, volunteer and guide at Bletchley Park, did a really good job of introducing each speaker. He was also one of the early members of the team striving to save Bletchley.

We were put up for a couple of nights in King's itself and, since I was then 91, Jack arranged for me to have special permission to park my car inside the courtyard near to our accommodation; it was very thoughtful of him.

My talk covered the subject of Lorenz and Tutte, and of course a bit of Turing as I always do, while everyone else spoke about Turing or computer history. Surprisingly, my talk was the only one to receive a standing ovation. Naturally, very few people had heard of Tutte's fascinating story and so it went down well.

A TALK AT BLETCHLEY PARK

Our second talk was at Bletchley Park on 30 June, two weeks after the event at King's College. For some years now, there has been a special tradition once a year to hold a Turing Day at the Park. The key element is the Annual Turing Lecture, and I was privileged to be invited to deliver this talk in 2012, as it was a very special one for Turing's centenary.

There were twelve speakers on the day, including an excellent introduction from Lord Charles Brocket. Charles was an ex-army officer and of course familiar with Bletchley Park and its role in the Second World War, but he had been horrified to find the site semi-derelict. Enquiries revealed that there was no public funding for it despite its national importance. Furthermore, much of the site had been cleared for housing development and it was assumed that the remainder would be bulldozed.

Charlie publicly pledged to veterans that he would fight this and in January 2009 submitted a written proposal for the first ever documentary that would reveal to the world the true role of Bletchley during the Second World War. As a result, the BBC commenced filming. Charles and Elm Street Media made the promo video. This was shown at Cannes, and finally a series of documentaries on aspects of the extraordinary achievements of the brains of Bletchley Park were screened during 2010. Charlie is still working on producing a compact one-hour video on the complete documentary about Bletchley, which can be included as part of the history taught at schools – such is the importance of the achievements at Bletchley.

For this event, it was a huge honour to be the main speaker. The tickets for the other speakers went on sale at £20 and included a half-day tour of Bletchley Park. My ticket was separate, at a cost of £50, and my talk was the last one, in the evening from 6:30 to 7.30 p.m., so the price included dinner. At first I was worried that the tickets were too expensive and that not enough people would be willing to spend so much money, but Jack was confident in me. It was sold out in a few days, and I was glad I could help raise some money to help Bletchley Park. At the dinner, I was surprised to see my GP, Dr Julian Bashforth, there. He had brought his parents with him, so his evening cost him £150 and he had come all the way from Petersfield in Hampshire. This was a really generous contribution to Bletchley Park.

Again, my talk went well and was the only one to receive a standing ovation. This was a really heart-warming experience, seeing the whole audience in front of me rise to their feet and break into warm applause. To have two such outcomes in a fortnight was extremely encouraging.

I was also glad to give my permission for my talk to the Annual Turing Lecture to appear in Jack's latest book, *The Turing Guide*, which consists of chapters from a group of specialist speakers. My final chapter was edited by Jack, and may be slightly altered, but I believe it will be Chapter 17, titled 'Tunny: Hitler's Most Secret Code'.

24

MEETING THE QUEEN AGAIN

SURPRISED AND DELIGHTED

I received a letter completely out of the blue in late November 2012, just after my 92nd birthday. The letter was from the Foreign & Commonwealth Office (Honours Committee) and the envelope was marked 'Strictly Personal, Official'. This letter informed me that I would be given an MBE in the forthcoming New Year's Honours List. This was a huge surprise, which I never expected. I was pleased to receive some acknowledgement after all these years and I thought that I would accept on behalf of those no longer around to receive it. I was also delighted at the prospect of meeting Her Majesty again after nineteen months.

On 28 February 2013 I had the pleasure of going to Buckingham Palace to receive my MBE award. To my surprise, Her Majesty recalled our first meeting, saying, 'I remember you, we met at Bletchley Park.'

I replied, 'Yes, ma'am, that was a red-letter day for us.'

Considering she meets so many people in a year, it was quite pleasing to have the Lorenz story recollected in this way. She talked for a few minutes, all the time with that beautiful smile. It was a very special moment to receive the award, but I cherished even more the occasion of meeting the Queen again. That day also happened to be mine and Mei's wedding anniversary. It was an extremely happy day indeed and one that we shall never forget.

Having said all that, I have mixed feelings: on the one hand, I was delighted, any honour is an honour and I cherish anything from the

Queen. On the other hand, I feel like I represent the other people in the Testery who worked on breaking Lorenz. They did an extremely important job and, in that sense, I feel that an MBE is not quite enough for that level of achievement. Despite Tutte's achievements having been declassified for more than a decade, he has received absolutely no recognition at all from our government. This is not because he emigrated to Canada and took Canadian nationality and so no longer counted as a Brit – this did not stop the British Royal Society giving him a fellowship when he was alive (a really outstanding award to mark his really outstanding achievement).

MY AWARD RECOMMENDED BY THREE MEN

I was pleased that the government had considered me for an honour. What I did not know is that any honour requires a recommendation from a minimum of three people. I am glad of an opportunity to thank these three friends, who kept me in the dark and recommended me to the Honours Committee. Without their thoughts and efforts, I would have had no honour and the government would have given me absolutely no recognition.

One of them was Julian Carey, who did such an excellent job with the BBC *Timewatch* programme in 2011. Here is his kind letter, dated April 2012. I hope Julian won't mind that I am taking this opportunity to share it with the public:

Dear Sir,

I would like to endorse and support the application for Captain Jerry Roberts (R.C. Roberts) to be granted an Honour in recognition of his amazing work at Bletchley Park during World War II.

I am a television producer for the BBC Wales and made the recent BBC 2 *Timewatch* film 'Codebreakers, Bletchley Park's Lost Heroes' (broadcast on 25 October 2011) which told the story of Bill Tutte and the breaking of Hitler's own personal code (known as the Lorenz or Tunny).

Breaking Lorenz is the great unsung success story of Bletchley Park. It gave the Allies unparalleled access to the highest level of intelligence and allowed them to read Hitler's personal reaction to the conflict as it unfolded. It provided everything from information on German troop strength and rations (across all theatres of the war) to exact defence plan and battle orders for pivotal clashes like Kursk and D-Day.

Jerry is the last surviving member of the team that broke the code and can recall personally deciphering the secret messages of the German High Command (including those of Hitler himself).

Jerry was one of the founder members of an elite group of code-breakers called 'The Testery' and a leading cryptographer. As a senior linguist and codebreaker who worked on Tunny (Lorenz cipher), he provided an invaluable contribution to the war effort.

One of the big parts of the Tunny story was that the code was so complex it prompted the invention of the world's first computer ('Colossus') to unravel it on a daily basis. But long before the machine was invented, the work was done by hand, by people like Jerry.

It's now been established that the Tunny break had an enormous impact on the Second World War, it undoubtedly helped shorten the war and has been singled out as a major factor in the success of D-Day. However due to the particular complexity of Lorenz / Tunny code and its strategic use after WW2 none of the men involved in breaking it were allowed to claim credit or talk about it.

Even after the story of Enigma became known, the facts about Tunny were considered too sensitive to reveal. The Enigma machine was based on pre-1940s technology and had been around since the 1920s. As such everyone knew what they were dealing with.

The Lorenz code was a bespoke system ordered by Hitler to be stronger, safer and provide more information than Enigma. The machine that engineered it was built in secret and not discovered until after the war. So throughout the break, the analysts at Bletchley Park were working completely in the dark. They had no machines to examine, no captured code books to refer to, nothing to work with except the new encrypted German messages. This is what makes the work of Jerry Roberts and his contemporaries all the more remarkable.

Because of the enforced silence over Tunny, most of Jerry's colleagues in the Testery passed away before the story broke and none of them ever received proper recognition.

For the last four years, Jerry has worked tirelessly to get their story out. He has also tried to raise public awareness of the important work of Bill Tutte and Tommy Flowers (the inventor of the Colossus).

It's worth mentioning that throughout his campaign Jerry has never looked for any personal recognition for his own work (which continued beyond Bletchley Park). He has only fought for the wider recognition of his team and throughout filming wanted to play down his part in this amazing story (any personal achievements had to be coaxed and cajoled out of him with a great deal of effort!).

Jerry is a hardworking, patriotic and very modest man. He is the kind of man who would never ask for any honour but I know he would be immensely proud to receive one, not least because he would see it as an award on behalf of all the men and women he worked alongside at Bletchley Park.

Jerry is now 92 and although he was bright and engaging when filming last year, he will not always enjoy this measure of good health. Indeed, he has become a little frail in the last few months despite the attention of his loving wife, Mei.

This is what has prompted me to write to you in support of this honour. I don't know how long the process may take or whether or not there is a fast-track system for special circumstances but as the last survivor of a remarkable team of people it would be wonderful to see Jerry rewarded in this way.

Thank you for your time.

Yours faithfully,
Julian Carey
Producer/Director. BBC Factual Programmes

The second recommendation was from my good friend and financial advisor, Brian Gonsalves, and the third was Lord Geoffrey Dear, who had heard my talk at UCL.

Before the award ceremony I read the official letter again. However, I noticed that the citation for my award said, 'This honour would be in recognition of your services to promoting the work of Bletchley Park'. I was confused and a bit puzzled by this. Their letter only mentioned 'promoting', and there appeared to have been no consideration given to my wartime service contribution at all. I did not only 'promote' the work of Bletchley Park – far more than that. In fact, I was a cryptographer! I regard myself as being the representative of my fellow codebreakers in the Testery. In that sense, I felt that this award under-valued the tremendous work they did during the war.

When I rang the Cabinet Office to put this to them and to give further background to the Honours Committee, I was told this award only related to my efforts in promoting Bletchley Park in recent years, not to my wartime service! I was also told that I would have to wait another five years if I turned down this honour. I was 92 already, so this was not a real possibility and I was genuinely disappointed. They would not consider any type of situation on an individual basis.

After a few days, I got an official letter from the Foreign & Commonwealth Office informing me that they had accepted my suggestion and altered the citation so that it reads, 'For services to promoting the work of Bletchley Park and to codebreaking'. They explained that the intelligence services are not accounted for at all and are not given any special awards. My wartime services were something they could not discuss at this time and they did not relate to the award in any way.

Of course, at the time no one undertook their war effort in order to receive any award; none of us would have been thinking about such things. There was work to be done and we just got on with it and did it to the best of our ability. Today, I feel this honour should be shared by a remarkably large number of other people.

For the last five years I have been working to gain better recogni-tion for the remarkable wartime achievements at Bletchley Park and ensure it is not forgotten. I worked tirelessly and travelled extensively to raise awareness of the successful work undertaken. I did not do this to receive an award. I was delighted to receive an honour, but it could have been better – not because we are fixed on titles – but in a gesture to those other guys in the Testery.

On 21 December, I received another formal letter from the Honours Committee which further explained to me, 'The Honours Committee were very aware of your wartime service but given the passage of time since 1945 were unable to take this fully into account in recommending the award or looking at the level of the award.'

I did receive a nice message from the lady who deals with the problems and questions for the Honours Committee. She wrote very positively:

Dear Jerry. Thank you for your email with all the complimentary media coverage concerning your MBE Honour, which reflects the esteem and respect of anyone who understands just how important your wartime work at Bletchley Park was for the Nation. It is only unfortunate that the Appointments Office failed to acknowledge or recognise the full significance of the wartime work carried out at Bletchley Park by you and the other very select members of the Testery. Rest assured that all of us who know and admire your work are delighted that you have been Honoured by the Queen, even though we are concerned that the level of the Honour could – and should – have been more substantial.

CONGRATULATIONS

After the New Year's Honours List was published on 29 December 2012, I was particularly pleased to receive so many congratulations from family and friends (some of whom I have not been in contact with for years), from friends at Bletchley Park itself and from many people whom I did not know personally.

One of the very first people to congratulate me was Sir John Scarlett, the chairman of Bletchley Park, with his heart-warming words:

Dear Jerry, I will be writing a proper letter, but wanted to send a quicker message to say how very pleased I am at the award of an MBE in the New Year Honours List. Please accept my warm congratulations. It is fascinating to see the interest the award has provoked, not to mention the splendid photograph in The Times. I think you are handling the interviews very well. It is hard to see this as appropriate recognition for the brilliant teamwork on Tunny. But it is a form of long overdue recognition all the same. And the public reaction certainly is. But the award formally acknowledges the hard work and strong commitment you have put in and demonstrated in recent years to the restoration of Bletchley Park. I know how important this is and, along with my fellow Trustees, are very grateful for all you continue to do.

Iain Standen, the CEO at Bletchley Park, also sent a lovely letter:

Dear Jerry, very many congratulations on behalf of both myself and all the staff at Bletchley Park on your award of an MBE in the New Year's Honours List. This is fitting of your tireless work to promote the Park and the crucial work performed by you and your colleagues here during the Second World War. We are very grateful for your effort because without advocates such as you, Bletchley Park would not enjoy the high profile it currently has and its future would be much less certain. Please enjoy the stardom and I am sure all your family and friends are, as are we all, hugely proud of you. May I wish you a prosperous New Year and I look forward to seeing you and Mei here at Bletchley Park again in the not too distant future. Fantastic news, many congratulations!

Those were very generous comments and wonderful letters and they mean a lot to me. These top leaders at Bletchley Park valued the contribution that I made during the war and recognised also the work that I have done to raise awareness of Bletchley Park's historic achievements. Over the last few years, doing things to help Bletchley Park has been a constant source of interest and satisfaction, although gaining recognition for Tutte and the Testery still has a long way to go. I am getting on a bit now, but still try to do my best. In recent years, Bletchley Park has become quite successful and in part this is due to the efforts of the new leadership.

I was overwhelmed that so many wonderful people sent me their congratulations and comments. A number of MPs, local newspapers and magazine reporters, the BBC, the national newspapers, radios, TV and online commentators were phenomenal with their comments. I was very moved by the whole event which was extraordinary and completely unexpected. I was really busy for a week or so, but I am very grateful to everyone for their very kind moral support.

NEWS, TV, RADIO AND INTERVIEWS

When the New Year's Honours List was published, the power of the media was phenomenal. I became a sort of celebrity overnight! For a few days I was really busy indeed. I had four television crews that all arrived at the same time to my doorstep for an interview: BBC News, Sky News, Channel 4 and ITV were all in our sitting room, taking interviews and getting my reaction to the award. I also had five radio interviews on the same day. We had a lot of emails and phone calls from the family, friends and other people; it was all very encouraging and exciting for a number of days.

In addition to those TV interviews, I gave a number of interviews for other media outlets. One that I vividly remember was with Adrian Goldberg from BBC Radio 5. His questions were very intelligent, for which he must have prepared thoroughly beforehand. We spoke for about twenty minutes. Our conversation is still available to listen to on the BBC website (see the links at the end of the book).

The publication of the New Year's Honours List elicited many comments from the public about the fairness of my award. Friends told me that my story featured in newspapers and on websites with one of my wartime photos taking up most of a page in *The Times*. They also told me that for a time the story was among the top ten most popular stories on the BBC website and a number of other websites too. I was amazed. This publicity allowed the story to reach an even larger audience.

There were 123 awards from the sporting world in the New Year's Honours List. Of course, Bradley Wiggins, a brilliant sportsman on his bike, got a knighthood. All the media coverage led to comparisons between our respective honours, provoking many comments. Some websites had to remove my stories and photos, while others had my photos covering the whole page; I can imagine the former was because it caused too many arguments.

Piers Morgan summed it all up on his Twitter feed. He wrote, 'Hmm … Riding a bike (Wiggo) – knighthood. Being Cherie Blair – CBE. Cracking Hitler's secret codes to save Britain (Jerry Roberts): MBE.' I found this quite amusing!

One of the BBC commentators wrote to me:

I know the BBC would like to come and film with you in the next couple of weeks, following the brouhaha about the honour. I gather there was a lot of reaction from the public, comparing your MBE with Bradley Wiggins. I am reminded of the first time I met and interviewed you in 2009, when you cited – very modestly – a woman who'd been honoured for running a chip shop!

Another email comment from a friend:

Many congratulations on your well-deserved New Year's Honour which, sadly, does not reflect the true value of your highly secret wartime service at Bletchley Park since it fails to appreciate or even acknowledge the uniquely important nature of your personal code-breaking work during very critical stages of World War ll. This very sensitive work was only declassified a few years ago, the citation comments from the Honours Committee is at best a pathetic excuse and at worst a complete travesty of common sense.

A friend sent me a copy of newspaper, a letter to the press from Dr David Barnett, who wrote to the editor:

Honours List award an utter disgrace. Unfortunately, the level of award granted to Captain Raymond Clark (Jerry) Roberts of Liphook in this year's Honours List was an utter, utter disgrace.

Captain Roberts was one member of the very, very small team of highly skilled and immensely valuable and immensely successful codebreakers working at Bletchley Park during the Second World War. This team significantly helped our century and its allies win the war and in doing so they rid the world of that wretched tyrant, Adolf Hitler.

Most graciously, Captain Roberts accepted his MBE on behalf of all his other codebreaking colleagues at Bletchley, but surely his award should have been a knighthood and not an MBE.

I was moved that so many wonderful people from the public sent their thoughts and comments to share with me. I wondered why my award was so popular?

I have learned a lot from this event by now, which I never expected. I have to 'keep calm and carry on' – as usual, my natural character. But there must be someone somewhere who is ignoring public opinion and has failed to properly recognise the achievements. I wonder what the Honours Committee are doing all day? I think most people in this country do understand, but we could have no words to describe it. However, my honour did raise the public opinion substantially about my situation, they could have dealt with it at the beginning. So far the government have paid little or no recognition to the great British men such as Alan Turing, Bill Tutte and Tommy Flowers. In fact, we all owe them a great debt.

25

INTERVIEWED BY KATHERINE LYNCH

Katherine Lynch, media director of the Bletchley Park Trust, seemed to have a very positive attitude. She used to be a journalist and reporter for the BBC, and rang me one day and left a message on my home phone.

When I rang her back, to my surprise she told me that she had interviewed me before and heard the fascinating Lorenz story when the Duke of Kent visited Bletchley Park in 2009. Ever since she had been interested and wanted to know more about it. I was impressed that she still remembered me, and I was pleased that someone had come along who was interested in the Lorenz story, and hopeful that Bletchley Park would now help me to further promote it.

Katherine did an excellent job on the story of Lorenz. She started interviewing me in order to be produce articles on the Bletchley Park website and its podcast. She also introduced me to her various contacts in the media. I was quite busy and exhausted, but excited and grateful indeed.

Katherine was the first person from Bletchley Park who took the initiative formally to interview me twice at my home in Hampshire. It's a long way from where she lives, but she was keen to grasp first-hand the real importance of what happened in the Testery with the breaking of Lorenz. She realised that there was a great opportunity since the story had never been completely revealed at Bletchley Park. It seemed clear to her that the story had historical importance and needed to be told.

The first interview with Katherine occurred at the end of January 2013, after the MBE had just been published. I remember it was cold and had snowed heavily for days. Despite the weather, she and Mark Cotton duly arrived. It took them four hours to get to my house because of delays with the trains at the time. Katherine brought Mark with her because he was an experienced audio engineer and musician who had done so much good work for Bletchley Park as a volunteer and had recorded many veterans' talks already. It was Mark who created the podcast for Bletchley Park – an invaluable step forwards in communicating with the public.

After six months, in July, Katherine and Mark came to interview me for a second time. This time they brought a friend, David, a cameraman from the BBC, so the three worked together to get further statements from me.

After the interviews, Mark made a number of podcasts from the recording to put on the Bletchley Park website and Katharine wrote an article appeared on the news section of the Bletchley Park website on 5 February 2013. Katherine is not just a quality reporter but also a brilliant writer. Here are some excerpts from her interview:

Captain Jerry Roberts is as passionate as ever an advocate of his colleagues at Bletchley Park. He told the Bletchley Park Trust: 'We have these three men whom I call the three heroes of Bletchley Park, Turing, Tutte and Tommy Flowers. Turing stopped not just Britain but Europe from being plunged into 50 years of a Nazi dark age. Tutte helped greatly to shorten the war. Tommy Flowers has laid the foundation of everything that's happened in the computer world internationally. These were great men and they've not been treated like great men. They did great things, achieved great things. I would like to suggest a joint statue on that fourth plinth in Trafalgar Square. That's if David Beckham doesn't mind.'

Captain Roberts says he was 'quite astonished' when the veil of secrecy was lifted from his and his colleagues' work breaking Lorenz, just ten years ago. He said 'For all that length of time I hadn't thought about Bletchley Park at all. It hadn't crossed my mind. It was just something that had happened in the dim and distant past, almost to somebody else.' He says his time at Bletchley was very special. 'The fact that you couldn't tell anybody about it and the fact that from what you'd seen you realised it was so confidential and so important, it was strange not to be able to talk about it and of course I didn't.' In 2002, when the secret of how the codebreakers cracked Lorenz was revealed, Captain Roberts was finally able to tell his wife, Mei, what he'd done. He says 'Mei knew I had worked at Bletchley Park but I hadn't told her what I'd worked on – Lorenz that was still classified. So I didn't tell her. We're very close, we tell each other everything. Well, nearly everything.'

The information being sent via the Lorenz system was often strategic rather than operational as it was the advanced system used by Hitler and the High Command. Captain Roberts says 'I remember today the excitement when we broke the first message with his signature on, great excitement. And then indeed when I broke my first message signed by him. It really was special.' He added 'In any case, we were breaking Lorenz on an almost industrial scale. The five links – three Russian links, the West and Italy – they all used different sets of wheel patterns. From 1st January 1944 onwards, they changed them almost every day. An edict had gone out which said you must change the patterns every day. And those patterns we in the Testery had to break every day.'

Captain Roberts says they were usually expected to break into a day's settings within an eight-hour shift. 'Sometimes it would be tough and difficult. In that case often they stayed on until they'd broken it because they couldn't give up. Other times they'd feel they hadn't got far enough and they'd leave it to someone else on the next shift.' He says Peter Hilton summarised well the feeling of getting a break, when Captain Roberts saw him seven or eight years ago. 'He said it was the most exciting thing he'd ever done in his life.'

He says locking the secrets away at the end of the war was not as difficult as we may imagine today. 'I was helped by the next job I did. The Army switched me to something totally different. It's difficult to imagine anything less similar, because with the War Crimes Investigation Unit you were driving round everywhere in a car to find the informants. At Bletchley you just sat on your bottom with a piece of paper and a pencil.'

He describes Bill Tutte as a rather slow-moving, slow-speaking man.

'I have a mental image of him, staring into the middle distance, twiddling his pencil and making counts on reams of paper. I used to wonder whether he was getting anything done. My goodness, he was. He was breaking Tunny.'

'It was as though we were from different tribes. We spoke different languages but were quite friendly. He was a mathematician, I was a linguist codebreaker. He hadn't the slightest interest in the German language and I was out of my depth with the mathematics. We exchanged the time of day but not much more because his nature was very different from mine.'

Capt Roberts says he didn't realise at the time what Tutte had achieved. 'The Lorenz system encrypted the text not once, not twice but three times. I would think it is almost unique that anybody had broken something with three levels of encryption.' He says about Bill Tutte 'His achievement was astonishing. What I don't understand is that any other country would be proud of these people and would cry their achievements from the rooftops. Cryptographers who did things sometimes more important than Montgomery did get nothing.' He says 'Turing got a bonus of £200 and an OBE. Unbelievable. Tommy Flowers got an innovation award of £1,000. He had to set himself up while people like Bill Gates made fortunes. And Tutte [was given] absolutely nothing, to this day. It's a national scandal. General Eisenhower said after the war that Bletchley decrypts shortened the war by at least two years. Ten million people died each year in the war.'

About his MBE, he says 'Any honour is an honour. The opportunity to meet Her Majesty again is a great bonus. Having said that I don't even mind if I don't get one – I lived without one for 92 years. But I feel I represent the Testery and they did a fantastic job. And an MBE is not a fantastic decoration.'

Captain Roberts believes people can only gradually come to appreciate the diverse and complex nature of what was achieved at Bletchley Park. 'I think people will learn slowly, but I've done my best to make it happen fast.'

'For me the big question is not how clever were you, it's did it make a difference? And it made a huge difference.'

PART FIVE

MY PERSONAL LIFE AND INTERESTS

26

KNOWING MEI

For the last twenty years I have been happily married to Mei, with whom I share a peripatetic life commuting between our homes in London and Hampshire. Everything we do together is joyous.

Our relationship happened as the leaf in the stream of my life took me to another lucky accident, when I was 68. I had been living in Westminster, at 58 Ebury Street, in a flat that I had owned since 1962 and used as my office, from where I had set up both my companies in the early 1970s. Across the corner was an Italian cafe restaurant run by two brothers, Andrew and John Fiori. The brothers had completely different characters: John was always friendly and liked to talk with his customers, and Andrew was more taciturn and serious. The cafe offered good food and had daily specials for lunch and, above all, a quick service. I used to go there quite regularly to have a quick lunch or a morning coffee as a break from my fairly pressured work. I would take my newspaper and, in the cheerful atmosphere of the Green Cafe, catch up on the news.

For well over a year, the cashier there had been a lady who was 30ish and from the Far East. She was quietly and crisply efficient and nice to the customers (although never too nice!), but I had never actually spoken with her and she had never talked with me. On one occasion, however, when I went across, the cafe was full and all the tables were occupied. Seated by herself at one was the cashier, who had just finished her shift and was having a cup of coffee before going home. I asked politely if I might join her and she agreed, so I put my coffee and newspaper down and we started chatting. The lady turned out to be Mei, an immigrant from Shanghai in the People's Republic of China. It turned out to be the most expensive cup of coffee I have ever bought in my life – but certainly the most worthwhile one.

We got to know each other a little better in the few weeks that followed and I gradually saw her more often. One evening, I bought two lamb chops and invited her to come across and cook them for us to have dinner together. We had a splendid dinner and made further progress in our relationship, but there was still no thought of anything more serious. I was not in any sense courting her, but just enjoying our pleasant friendship. I asked Mei what she liked doing and she replied that she enjoyed watching television in the evenings. So I bought a set of impressively sized televisions and a four-head recording machine, which I had installed in my office so that we could watch TV in the evening together.

Mei and I had an unusual situation; it seemed a ridiculous match and the odds against us were huge. We were of different nationalities (she came from the Far East and I was an Englishman), with a thirty-five-year gap between us. Our natures and professional lives had been completely different. She was an artist and book illustrator and I was a facts-and-figures marketing man. It could never work, forget it, don't even try …

Our relationship continued to grow and we became good friends. As time went on, Mei and I got to know each other a bit better. We went for walks in Green Park, and took our first photo together there. We went to the wonderful Chinese State Circus when it came to town – I still remember the fabulous performances we saw at Clapham Common. I asked Mei to visit Barcelona in Spain for the weekend, but she declined. She was still quite shy. I hadn't had a holiday for some time, so I again invited Mei to join me for a holiday, in the UK instead. We went to Bath and Stratford – Shakespeare's birthplace. We then went on one of my work visits to Hamburg in Germany and later Paris. This really sealed our friendship.

When I met Mei, I was genuinely fond of her. She was a highly interesting person, intelligent and attractive, and she could have chosen any of the younger men around. In those years, I always thought I had a complicated family situation and this often put me off going on dates, as I did not want to make it even more complicated. I was worried that Mei would inherit a bewildering family if we got married. Much to my surprise, she did not mind my past at all and got on well with some of my children.

Mei had established herself well in Britain; she was granted British citizenship long before our marriage. She came from Shanghai, where she had had a good fifteen-year career as an illustrator for the books and magazines in the biggest publishing house there. She had a perfectly good job but she decided to come to the UK to learn English. During that time, she took a part-time job. Soon after, she passed her driving test, followed by a year in St Martin's College of Art and Design in London, where she took her MA degree – all in the space of a couple of years before our marriage. She didn't need to marry me to become a British citizen or gain a better life. She has a great sense of independence, made her own way very successfully and could stand on her own two feet.

I was serious; I am old-fashioned and I did not want people to think I took advantage of her. I asked Mei whether we should get engaged. She agreed and I was delighted. Soon after that we got married and for our honeymoon we went to Barbados for a fortnight – a place I used to go for holidays when I worked in Venezuela.

It proved to be, indeed, third time lucky. Mei turned out to be the most wonderful wife I ever dreamed of, and I couldn't be happier. We have had a happy marriage and lived together for more than twenty years. Even though we live in each other's pockets and see each other every minute of every day, a very taxing situation normally, it has worked out for us perfectly. Given the amount of time we spend together, our marriage would be the equivalent to fifty years for many couples, and I can't thank Mei enough for the pleasure she has brought into my life – she has helped to keep me going.

So, what is the secret of our marriage success? Quite simply, we speak openly and honestly about everything so there is no mistrust. Mei lived by the traditional Chinese philosophy of respecting people. She often says, 'I was taught since childhood to respect parents, teachers and any elders.' Putting the other's interest before your own is a great virtue and one we have adhered to. A pleasure shared is a pleasure doubled; a trouble shared is a trouble halved – I have kept these fundamental principles close to my heart, and our marriage has truly transformed my life. A loving couple should get on well and share everything happily, making every day worthwhile.

KNOWING MORE ABOUT CHINA

Before knowing Mei, I was already interested in China and read quite bit about Chinese cultures and history. I was fascinated by Mei's family and her background. In the summer of 2000, we visited Shanghai and I met her parents for the first time. We visited a number of ancient places in the north of China and had a lovely two weeks' holiday. Chinese people are very hospitable; the whole family would get together for meals quite often. Mei's parents and three brothers made me very welcome. Her parents married when they were aged 19 and 18 – an 'arranged marriage' agreement was made between their parents; it was not a 'love match'. Amazingly, their marriage lasted more than sixty years before their deaths.

One of Mei's brothers, Moto, was a businessman, running his own companies very successfully. After Moto visited us a couple of times, we had the opportunity to do business with China. His company was progressing fast in the field of industrial electrical products, and he gave us the opportunity to handle trade deals in the UK as its sister company. Since I had considerable business experiences, having successfully run my own companies, and since Mei could speak Chinese and I could speak four of Europe's languages, we were very happy to handle this. Mei and I soon set up a new company to perform the export and import in the mid 1990s. This was a pleasant and profitable situation. It was quite an education dealing with people in both the Eastern and Western worlds, and we made a lots of business friends. After ten years or so, I started to get involved with Bletchley Park activities, because I knew Lorenz was just declassified, and Mei and I took on a new journey of responsibilities ahead.

Although we don't always understand each other's languages, Mei and I get on well with a kind sense of humour and we have a lot of laughter together. I greatly regret that I am not able to speak Chinese. I have considered learning, but at my age it is pretty difficult to pick it up. Chinese is a very complex language. Mandarin is totally different from English. Its four tone levels, where the same sound intoned at different levels can have quite different meanings, means every word can be interpreted differently depending upon how it is spoken. I was quick at mastering four European languages, but Chinese is so different – particularly writing in Chinese; I found it completely daunting. I have nine or ten words of Chinese that I can use confidentally, and I occasionally bring this up to impress people. I could say, for example, Hello (ni hao), How are you? (ni hao ma?) and of course Cheers (gang bei). The trouble was I couldn't understand the answer, not to any great effect!

I have a personal reason to be grateful for a Chinese doctor. For more than twenty years, I suffered from persistent pain in my back and shoulder. My doctors told me I had arthritis and prescribed pills and painkillers, but it did not help. The trouble was instead cured by Mei's friend Professor Wang Ning-Sheng a leading Chinese medicine doctor who came from Nanjing. He gave me acupuncture and massages with herb oil on my shoulder and back. Each session lasted one hour, twice a week for five months. Professor Wang explained that the muscles in that area had atrophied and needed to be brought back to life. When he had to go back to China, he sent me a month supply of herb medicine from China. Mei cooked these herbs for me to drink every day for a month, and the pain gradually disappeared, as Professor Wang had predicted. Ten years on, there has been no further twinge. I was completely cured; it is quite remarkable. On another occasion, my GP at a clinic in London had warned me that I might have trouble with my heart, but Professor Wang felt my pulse in his own special way and looked at my tongue carefully before declaring that I had a good sound heart and no problem at all. I wanted to be sure, so I went to a Harley Street specialist who tested me by hanging a special machine on my neck for twenty-four hours. It turned out my heart was indeed quite normal. This was another example of Professor Wang's extraordinary knowledge. These experiences taught me how wonderful Chinese medicine can be in a totally different way from Western medicines. I am totally convinced that the 2,000 years of Chinese doctor and herb medicine has developed into its own magic.

27

MY FAMILY AND PREVIOUS MARRIAGES

I had not been so lucky with my previous two marriages. My first marriage was to Elizabeth in the early 1950s. When I met her, she had been widowed with a daughter, Karen, aged 4, who would become my stepdaughter. Elizabeth's husband had been an airman who died in the Second World War. She wished to marry me and my heart went out to her. We went on to have a daughter, Alexandria.

Elizabeth and I did not have much in common, especially when I was very busy running my own companies in the early 1970s. I thought we could have weathered through and the situation would improve, but for twenty years it was strained. After the divorce, I still carried on with my responsibility of being the best daddy I could and financially supported Elizabeth and both children.

My second wife, Rosanne, came along in the 1970s. She was a member of staff at one of my businesses and we knew each other only a few months, got married and soon after we had two children, Ian and Dora. I also had two stepchildren, Sarah and Ruya, from Rosanne's side. The marriage lasted only a few years before Rosanne died of a sudden heart attack. At the time she lived in Wales, in a house I had bought for her; it was a place she was very fond of.

Rosanne's death left me in a very difficult situation, but I did my best in bringing up the four children. I always split my time as best I could, spending every evening at home with them and shopping and cooking for them every weekend. Sarah and Ruya were teenagers at the time. Ruya left home and became independent, while Sarah stayed and supported me in looking after the two youngsters.

I had to be the loving father and provide all the financial means, which included sending Dora to a private boarding school in Dorset for six years to ensure she got the best education and was happy there, while still making sure she got to see the family. I would drive for five hours every weekend to pick her up from school and bring her back home to Barnes while I was still engaging with my own companies. For fourteen years I was a single parent and had no one to share my own feelings with, whether happiness or sadness. Life was very hectic and no one can be prepared for situations like that. As a result, I had given up on love and could not think about women or marrying again – until Mei.

Mei's only child, Chao, joined us when she was 12. She went to a girls' comprehensive school in Westminster called The Grey Coat Hospital, where she made huge progress in the first year. She was given a prize every year after that for a number of years, which made us very proud. She then went on to do a four-year degree course in German at UCL. I was pleased to see that she followed in my footsteps. She speaks fluent German and now uses the language in her profession.

Today, the family has truly grown and expanded. I have eight grandchildren, all in their 20s and 30s and doing extremely well, most of them artists and musicians. Sarah's son, Robin, went to Latymer Upper School, where I had studied many years ago, and he is currently studying engineering at Cambridge University. I am immensely proud of them all.

One thing I always felt enormously painful about was that my mother died in 1976 aged 83, and sadly, both my parents died without knowing about the important secret work I had been doing during the war. They must have known I had been doing well when they saw me promoted to captain at a young age, but I could not tell them any details as it was not to be declassified for another forty-two years after my father died in the early 1960s. My younger brother Frank didn't know either; he died in his early 40s, as he had always been a rather sickly child. My elder brother Arnold, was the only person who knew about it when I told him a few years ago after Lorenz was declassified. He died, aged 96 in 2009.

28

HOBBIES AND INTERESTS

Mei and I surprisingly shared the same interests – almost everything, even the same programmes on television. We were quite the opposite in the beginning, but we both have a positive attitude and respect for each other that brought our life together. Over the years, Mei and I have developed quite a wide range of interests, including investment, gardening and properties. We have had busy lives and always had things to do, but most of the time we like to work together as a team. We are indeed very fortunate to have each other.

Investment bonds provide a daily element of interest and stimulation. We have followed the financial market day-by-day for the last eighteen years now. We monitor financial news before deciding where to invest our portfolio and whether to make any changes. This fits into the pattern of thinking that Mei and I have developed. We have always been keen with whatever we own to develop it. You have to see the potential, work at it and find your direction to make your success happen – but there is always some element of risk there. In cryptography, some people look at a text and see opportunities, while others see nothing. To some extent that is true of investments as well.

Property is another area in which we have engaged. Initially, it was Mei's idea. She enjoys investing her fund in property and renovating it, then selling it on or renting it out to make a profit. Our first fling came about when Mei read an advertisement for a good-looking Victorian terraced house in Plymouth. She bought it at an auction in London for the sum of £29,000, without having even seen it. However, I thought this property was too risky and too far away to keep an eye on in the long term, so we refurbished the house inside and out to make it look fresh, as it had been a little neglected. We were able to sell it – we received two offers in a week once it was on the market – with a useful gain. But in fact this was a very foolish thing to do, as in few years we could have made a further substantial profit. It was I who urged Mei to sell it, and I have never been forgiven for doing so! The experience, however, showed the way forward.

My interest in music, however, was developed during my time at Bletchley Park. I found I had time on my hands in the evenings when I was off-duty at the Park. To fill this time I bought myself a good radio (I think it was a Pye) and I started to listen to the news and the talk programmes. I also began to listen to concerts of classical music, and very quickly began to take great enjoyment in this. I could recognise a few of the classical masterpieces, and I found it relaxing and enjoyable after a busy day's concentration. Though my taste covered the nineteenth century, from Beethoven to Sibelius, I had little or no taste for twentieth-century classical music. Sibelius particularly appealed to me; he seems to have created his own branch of music, quite different from the traditional nineteenth-century style one heard from Beethoven, Schubert or Brahms. It evokes his homeland of Finland. Largely, it's snowy, lonely, icy deserts, with large forests of fir trees contrasting against the white. Very occasionally there were chamber concerts at Bletchley Park, and I went to one or two of these to become acquainted to this unfamiliar branch of music and they added a great deal to my overall enjoyment of music. We never had any visits by orchestras at Bletchley Park – one had to go up to London to the Royal Albert Hall for these. Later, when I went to live in New York, I bought a gramophone and a lot of records to play on it. This was brought back with me to Britain and I still have it.

Another interest in my life is antique furniture; today most of my furnishings are from the eighteenth century, with a few from the early nineteenth century. I got the bug when I lived at Leatherhead, Surrey, in the 1950s, not far from a small centre of antique furniture shops, in Dorking High Street. I found it fascinating to speculate about the family who might have previously owned the pieces over the centuries, or who had had the pieces made for them 200 years ago, in very different circumstances from today.

One of my oldest hobbies, begun when I was a child of 10, is collecting stamps. Over the course of five or six years in my early teens, I built quite an interesting collection, though it was of no great value. There is tremendous variety in the range and subjects stamps illustrate and you can learn a lot by looking at them. Every now and then, I get the stamp books out and look at them, and they give a great deal of pleasure and bring back many old memories. There was however a completely different development that arose on this front. Some time in early 2012, I was contacted by Tony Buckingham. He and his wife Cath run a company called Buckingham Covers which specialises in the handling of First Day Covers (FDCs) and stamp collectors' gifts. He had seen Julian Carey's programme and the BBC *Timewatch* programme about the Lorenz story, in which I appeared, and he wanted to put my story on his beautiful FDC envelopes. The front had a picture of Bletchley Park and a set of lovely stamps on it. On the back of envelopes was my story in brief. In this way, I was again able to help achieve better recognition for my colleagues and the Lorenz story. I was so glad when he gave me a set of these three envelopes as a souvenir to add to my collection. He also asked me to sign a number of other envelopes for him, which he would then sell on at a special price to the collectors. Part of the proceeds from this were to be given to charity. I signed batches of fifty or so a number of times for him and donated all this money to my old school, Latymer.

Sport is another love of mine. At school, I was able to play cricket with my classmates but not football. I suffered from asthma, and having to run about on a cold winter's day brought out the worst in this. However, I played cricket every summer. I prospered at cricket and became captain of cricket at Latymer in the late 1930s. Even after I left the school, I used to play for the old Latymarians. Nowadays, of course, at the age of 93, I couldn't get around to playing either and I have to be content with watching it on TV. I enjoy watching tennis, golf and other key games of interest. This includes rugby and football. I always support Wales in this. My family came originally from Wales and I feel to a certain extent Welsh myself, even though I was born in London. It was a matter of joy when Wales won the Six Nations Championships a few years ago. What is quite extraordinary is a nation which has about three million inhabitants can rise to such heights. Not only sports but also I love to watch *Countdown* every weekday in the afternoon on Channel 4, and the History Channel.

Reading is one of my favourite pastimes; I have loved it since I was a child of 10 or 11. In my later years, I have been able to read in other European languages – French, German and Spanish. I particularly like history, but also poetry from the nineteenth century, including the Romantic poets; they still give constant pleasure. However, more recently I developed macular degeneration, which means I have to have regular monthly treatments on my eye. This treatment is a new technique; I had to pay for the first two years as it was not provided on the NHS in the early days. The injection for the eye is a godsend. There is a certain limitation, but I was still able to carry on reading and writing and see things over the last few years until very recently. I owe many thanks to Mr Nicolas Lee, an eye specialist consultant at the Western Eye Hospital. Without his treatment and care, I would have been blind for a few years. I greatly appreciate the help from the NHS.

Given my eye condition and my old age, this book is a substantial amount of work, so Mei and I have come up with a simple solution – I dictate into a small machine and she organises the typing. I am very lucky to have the help necessary to get this book down on paper.

AFTERWORD

The breaking of Lorenz by the British at Bletchley Park is one of the greatest achievements in the history of cryptography. It brought so many benefits to the British nation and, indeed, to Europe as a whole.

Bletchley Park was an extremely important place during the Second World War, and its work was inspired. At the time, it was one of the most secret establishments in the country. Bletchley Park was not only the home of cryptographers breaking the enemy's codes and ciphers that helped the Allies win the war, but was also the birthplace of the computer.

I realised at the time that I was working on an important task, but I did not see that as clearly as I do today, when we know so much more about the effects of our work. With everything pulled together, it was quite an amazing achievement. Without the three heroes, Alan Turing, Bill Tutte and Tommy Flowers; without the Testery breaking Lorenz messages successfully; and without the many other supporting personnel at Bletchley Park, Britain and the rest of Europe would be a very different place today. We owe a lot to these people and their names should be raised in the consciousness of the public. The UK should be very proud of them.

APPENDIX

LIST OF TESTERY PERSONNEL

Towards the end of the war in 1945, I kept a copy of the original list of personnel of the Testery, with the name of all 118 staff on it. If I had been caught at the time, I could have been in serious trouble, but it has been an invaluable document in recent years. I have been able to help people's relatives to identify their loved ones. It is also a vivid reminder of many of my colleagues from so many years ago.

THE THREE SHIFTS OF THE TESTERY, 1945

	9 a.m.–4 p.m.	4 p.m.–12 a.m.	12 a.m.–9 a.m.
ROOM 41 (Cryptographers)	Capt. Ericsson (Peter)	Capt. Roberts (Jerry)	Mr Masters (Victor)
	CSM Barratt	S/Sgt Philips	Capt. Dobbins
	Lieut Levenson	S/Sgt Denman	Capt. Davies
	R.S.M. Wild	Mr Christie	Capt. Jenkins (Roy)
	S/Sgt Holmes	Mr Thompson	Sgt Rollo
	Sgt Uphill		Mr Edgerley
	Mr Michie		Sub. Worsley
	CSM Pollard		
	Permanently on days – Major Oswald, Capt. Marshall, RSM Benenson, Mr Colvill (General Manager), Mr Hilton (Peter)		
ROOM 40 (Wheel setting)	Sgt Mayo-Smith	Capt. Wesson	Mr Jones
	Sgt Gloster-Downing	Capt. Maddocks	Capt. Bancroft
	Cpl Porter	RSM Roots	Capt. Potts
	Cpl Rees	SSM Walford	Sgt Cook
	Cpl Williams	SQMS Garner	Cpl Rogers
	Cpl Ramsey	Cpl Mashiter	Cpl Keyte
	L/Cpl Nash	Cpl Cook	L/Cpl Langford
	L/Cpl Bradley	L/Cpl Taylor	Cpl Maskell
	Permanently on days – Sub. Bridgwater, Cpl Saward, Cpl Street		
ROOM 28	CSM Colling	Sub. Palmer	Sub. Tickle
	Mr Wood	Mr Jeeves	Capt. Winter
	S/Sgt Collings	Sgt Beckingham	
ROOM 29	Lt Van Der Wal	Cpl. Peterson	CSM Carney
	Cpl Ashworth	Sgt Alderton	
	Permanently on days – Capt. Hayward		
ROOM 27 (Decoding staff)	S/Sgt Gutteridge	Sgt Godsell	S/Sgt Traynor
	S/Sgt Owen	Sgt Sproston	Sgt Hampson
	Sgt Smith	Cpl Cook	Cpl Jaques
	Cpl Mollier	Cpl Eccleston	Cpl Witty
	Cpl Roberts	Cpl Bell	Cpl Davies
	Cpl Wright	Cpl Dorney	Cpl Leverett
	Pte Charlesworth		
	Pte Dean		
	Under Instruction – L/Cpl Holloway		
ROOM 43	Permanently on days – Cpl Hickman, Cpl Sayr		
ROOM 12 (Registration)	SQMS Finch	Cpl Daniels	SQMS Sinclair
	Cpl Enderby	Cpl Gwyne	Sgt Smith
	Cpl Swadling	Cpl Fitel	Cpl Ansell
	L/Cpl Thomas	Cpl Smith	L/Cpl Bailey
BLOCK F	Cpl Marshall	Cpl York	Cpl Phillpot
	Pte Harwood		
ROOM 31	Cpl Ophen	Cpl Hart	Cpl Haddick
	L/Cpl Price	Cpl Marti	Cpl Horton
		Cpl Coons	
	Permanently on days – SSM Bloom, S/Sgt Wheeler, Sgt Maunsell, Cpl Gibbons, Cpl Spreadborough, Cpl Long		
	Statistics – Sgt Nathan, Cpl Cook, Cpl Aspinall		

USEFUL WEBSITES

1. What was Lorenz and how it works: video by James Grime and Claire Butterfield: www.youtube.com/watch?v=GBsfWSQVtYA
2. *Timewatch* programme Codebreakers: Bletchley Park's Lost Heroes: www.bbc.co.uk/programmes/p00l9j0v
3. *Science Britannica* programme by Brian Cox. Bill Tutte's work is featured in episode two: www.bbc.co.uk/programmes/p01d56f7
4. Bill Tutte memorial: billtuttememorial.org.uk/
5. Rory Cellan-Jones' interview, 2008: news.bbc.co.uk/1/hi/technology/7713003.stm
6. Interview with Andrew Webb in 2008: news.bbc.co.uk/1/hi/technology/8491227.stm
7. Jerry's UCL talk, 2009: www.ucl.ac.uk/news/news-articles/0903/09031601
8. Nicholas Witchell's interview when meeting HM the Queen: www.bbc.co.uk/news/uk-14164529
9. Adrian Goldberg's interview for New Year's honours lists: www.bbc.co.uk/news/uk-20863205
10. Tom Hepworth honours Jerry Roberts with stamps: www.bbc.co.uk/news/uk-england-22113297
11. Turing Centenary Lecture – Jerry's talk, 2012: audioboom.com/posts/1133623-turing-education-day-captain-jerry-roberts-part-1?t=0
12. Katherine's interview on the Bletchley Park podcast 2013: audioboom.com/posts/1239087-bletchley-park-podcast-extra-e17-capt-jerry-roberts-mbe-full-interview
13. Lord Charles Brocket's short film for Cannes Film Festival in 2010: www.youtube.com/watch?v=OqxDEm0BTw0
14. *General Report on Tunny*: codesandciphers.org.uk/documents/newman/newman.pdf
15. Saving Bletchley Park website by Dr. Sue Black: savingbletchleypark.org

INDEX